Elia Wilkinson Peattie, Railroad Company Northern Pacific

A Journey Through Wonderland

The Pacific Northwest and Alaska

Elia Wilkinson Peattie, Railroad Company Northern Pacific

A Journey Through Wonderland
The Pacific Northwest and Alaska

ISBN/EAN: 9783744761925

Printed in Europe, USA, Canada, Australia, Japan

Cover: Foto ©Andreas Hilbeck / pixelio.de

More available books at **www.hansebooks.com**

Through Wonderland;

OR

The Pacific Northwest and Alaska,

WITH

*A DESCRIPTION OF THE COUNTRY TRAVERSED BY THE
NORTHERN PACIFIC RAILROAD.*

BY

ELIA W. PEATTIE.

———

Rand Mᶜ Nally & Co.
CHICAGO

PRINTERS
AND
PUBLISHERS.

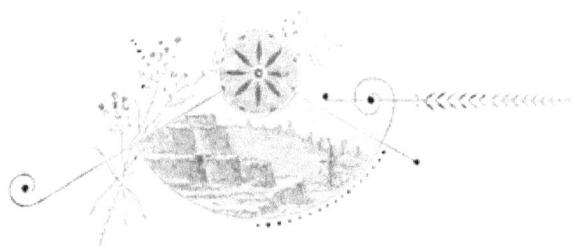

ILLUSTRATIONS.

DETROIT LAKE AND HOTEL MINNESOTA, DETROIT, MINN.

A Journey Through Wonderland.

I pity the man who can travel from Dan to Beersheba,
and cry, " 'Tis all barren!' "

—LAURENCE STERNE.

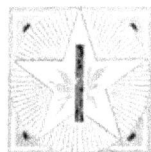

IT was the merest chance that took me westward. I had never
previously been 500 miles from New York—except, of course,
to Europe. Everyone goes to Europe. The chance that made
me journey westward was a business one; but other than business
reasons made me glad to go.

"If you ever get an ache of the heart," said a young Frenchman whom I
once met, "take a long journey. Visit the Indian Ocean, for instance. There,
wrapped in a pajama, one lies on deck at night, watching the swaying of the
masthead and the twinkling of the stars—the languorous stars of those latitudes.
Time, space, and peace are all there is left of life, and the bitterness and weari-
ness melt away from one, and seem to become a part of the mists in the blue
distance. Take my word for it, there is nothing like a voyage on some solitary
sea to cure the heartache."

Thus, when it came about that business took me to Duluth, to Winnipeg,
and St. Paul, I concluded to go farther—across the plains, the mountains, and
to Alaska. I substituted Alaska for the Indian seas. Alaska, I confess, seemed
a very long way off, for I had not, at that time, learned that distance is no actual
quantity, but is determined only by the convenience or inconvenience that
attends a journey. When I left my native city, however, the words "Duluth"
and "Winnipeg" were without significance to me, and even St. Paul meant
little enough.

The first two days are indistinct in my mind. There are circumstances
under which a man can not enjoy even a Niagara. I could not hear its roar for
the cooing of newly-married lovers, and considering a recent experience of mine,
I naturally felt irritated. A few long days on the lakes followed, and I got a
certain comfort out of them. It is true that I did not lie wrapped in my pajama
while fanned by tropical and perfumed breezes. There were no tropical
breezes, for one thing, and I had no pajama. As the oxygen got into my lungs,
the morbidity went out of my soul, and I should have been almost happy but for
a young lumberman on board. He was a good-natured young man—indeed,
he was too good-natured, for he never looked at me without smiling. There

(7)

was nothing ridiculous about me, of that I was sure.   I understood the subject
of clothes if any man in New York did, and it was hard for me to find out why
a man in a flannel shirt, and a hat at least three years in arrears of the fashion,
should laugh at me.

"I should like to see you," he used to remark, "after you have caught the
fever."

DINING CAR INTERIOR ON THE WONDERLAND ROUTE.

"What fever?" I anxiously inquired.

"Why, the western fever," he replied.   "You will get it, or my name is
Dennis."

The phraseology of this young lumberman was not always choice.   I was
not sorry when I learned that we were approaching Duluth, where I was likely
to escape him.

"Duluth," I said to myself, "is no doubt a chilly little harbor with a few lumber mills in the background, and fish-nets straggling on the beach." I had seen a great many dull hamlets of that sort, and I was not interested. To be sure, the young lumberman was buzzing facts in my ear with the pertinacity of a statistical mosquito, but they meant nothing to me.

"It is the largest grain-shipping port in the world," he informed me. "It has a population of 45,000, sir, and its grain elevators have an aggregate capacity of 12,000,000 bushels."

Then he spread his legs apart, and waited for me to be overcome with these facts; but the truth is, I have never been much impressed with figures. But when I saw Duluth rising ledge above ledge, I felt a sudden thrill of admiration. Southeast of this lay innumerable saw-mills, and their metallic humming came over the water.

"That," said my informant, "is West Superior and Superior City. It is no mean town taken together, even when compared with Duluth. Their population is a little less than half that of Duluth, but they are good towns, sir—good towns. Look at the coal docks, if you please, and you will not be surprised to hear that their coal receipts are over a million tons a year. They communicate with Duluth by the Northern Pacific bridge, you know. But Duluth is the town, sir! Founded on a rock, with seven railroads, ten banks; with coal, wheat, lumber, steel, railway cars to ship out—"

"My friend," I broke in wearily, "I know all that. I know that in 1870 there was nothing here but a sand-bank. Now I am quite willing to believe that it is the most civilized city on earth. I know also that you western gentlemen are accomplished orators."

My lumberman turned to me suddenly, and button-holed me.

"Look here," said he, "if you knew what you were talking about, I should get mad. But I think the time is coming when you will feel different. If the time comes when you have occasion to watch a town grow as I have this, you will know what it is to feel the same sort of pride. I have seen Duluth when she was nothing but sand and rock. Look at her now, sir! Beautiful homes stand on those terraces of trap; 12,500 miles of railroad are directly tributary to her; her taxable property is in the neighborhood of $30,000,000. Of course I am proud of Duluth—as proud as I would be of one of my own children. Never before in the history of the world has it been the privilege of men to watch the growth of cities as they can in the United States in the nineteenth century. And it seems to me, sir, to be one of the great privileges. You may not appreciate it, but I do."

What could I do but give a hearty hand-shake to the enthusiastic lumberman? In the two days I remained in the cities at the head of Lake Superior, to which I had been introduced with so memorable a eulogy, I experienced none of the lack of comfort and convenience that I had anticipated—indeed, I found conveniences that we in the East had not thought it worth while to provide ourselves with. It was in this town that I met a young man whom I was destined to see more than once in my journey. He was dressed from head to foot in corduroy, and was laden with a most remarkable quantity of fishing-tackle and gun-cases. I was on my way to St. Paul by way of Ashland, thinking it profitable to take that somewhat circuitous route for the sake of seeing that popular resort, when the corduroy-clad individual I speak of sat down opposite me, and loaded three seats with his paraphernalia. I saw that he was fixing a steady gaze on me, but supposing this to be a part of the rudeness I naturally expected to encounter in the West, I paid no attention to it, until at last he broke out with:

"My dear sir, I am sure from your physiognomy that you are a sportsman."

"Then my features belie me," I returned, curtly, "for I have neither the skill to bring down game nor the patience to hold a line."

"But it is impossible to deceive me," he protested. "I know a sportsman when I see one. Your skill may not be developed, and your passion for sport may be latent, but it exists, sir! It exists! And before we part, I hope to prove it to you."

"You are out, then, on a sporting expedition?" I inquired.

"I may say," he returned, crossing his corduroy legs, "that I never go on any other sort of an expedition, and I flatter myself that I have visited many of the most famous resorts of the sportsman in the known world; and I must say I have never found anything finer in the way of trout streams than up here on the north shore of Lake Superior. Gooseberry River, sir, is one of the most extraordinary streams! I caught one trout there that weighed—"

"Pardon me," I interrupted, "but what is your name?"

I gave him my card, bearing a name that I flattered myself was not without patriotic associations—Scott Key. His card, promptly tendered, showed in fine script the honest name of John Parke.

"When your latent capabilities in the way of sporting are developed," continued this amiable gentleman, "you must go to Deerwood. Deerwood is ninety-seven miles west of Duluth. You can get a good hotel over your head at night, and in the day you may wander through one of the most beautiful woods it was ever the privilege of man to set eyes on, and shoot anything worth the shooting, except a Bengal tiger. The deer are superb—and, what is better, they are frequent, so to speak. As for fishing, you can have anything you want. There is pike, sir, and black bass; there is muskallonge, whitefish, pickerel, croppies, sunfish, rock bass, bullheads—"

"I am afraid your eloquence is wasted on me," I protested, "for I do not know one sort of fish from another."

"Well!" pityingly exclaimed Mr. Parke, "I never knew a man who had been so wrested from his natural calling as you, sir. Whenever I look at you, I associate you with a trolling-spoon or a split bamboo rod and a brown hackle. You should go up to the Brule—only 35 miles from Duluth, on the Ashland line of the Northern Pacific—and throw a fly at some of the gamy trout there."

It is unnecessary to repeat more of what this young man said. I seemed to be destined to meet with enthusiasts.

I spent a day in Ashland, a most picturesque little town, the extreme eastern terminus of the Northern Pacific Railroad, lying on the silver Bay of Chequamegon, with the Apostle Islands visible. But although Ashland is a famous summer resort, and has a large hotel bearing the name of the bay, and especially adapted to midsummer tourists, its interest is not simply a romantic one. It is the largest shipping port of iron ore in the United States, and has steel manufactures, among its many other industries, where the ore from the Gogebic range is worked. The Wisconsin Central makes it its terminus. But I cared less for the material advantages than for those odorous forests of pine, those clear streams, and the bay, bright in the sunshine of the late summer.

I took the train to St. Paul, and arriving in that city busied myself with my duties. A man raised in a great metropolis could feel but little interest in so young and experimental a city as that I found myself in. At least this was what I told myself. But I had not been a day in the place before I began to feel something peculiar in the atmosphere. I am referring, so to speak, to the mental atmosphere. The men, for example, seemed to have a strange energy. They walked as if they had something particular to do, and but a very little time to do it in. I began to walk quicker myself, and to look about me with some degree of interest. The buildings, I soon saw, were of a newer and more artistic architecture than that usually seen in American cities.

St. Paul rises in proud terraces from the Mississippi, the first two devoted to business houses, the second two to the homes of the city. A fringe of gentle groves crowns the topmost heights, which bend to the sweep of the river, and here are those houses which I hear have made St. Paul famous in the West as a desirable residence city. I have a theory—not very sound, perhaps, from a commercial stand-point—that the true success of a city is gauged largely by its humane institutions, rather than by its number of bank buildings; though, indeed, the idea is not so far wrong, for it is only the prosperous city that will have hospitals and asylums, since they are only provided for after the jails, the court-houses, and the merchant houses are well established. I found three hospitals, two orphan asylums, and several other charitable establishments. In St. Paul the new county court-house has had a million dollars expended on it—a statement which I did not find it difficult to believe. There are eighteen public school-houses, at which 15,000 children are being educated. All these facts I did not learn at once, nor because I made any especial effort to discover them, but they were thrust upon me by patriotic citizens, and I transcribe them for the benefit of others. Six trunk lines of railroads, from the East, run into this city and through Minneapolis. Indeed, so closely are these two cities wedded, that, in the mind of the stranger, at least, it is difficult to separate one from the other.

"I have always been distressed at the rivalry that some persons have forced into existence between St. Paul and Minneapolis," said a well-known judge, whose office was in one city, and his home in the other.   "The time is not far distant when these two cities will be united by a continuous line of suburbs, as they now are by commercial interest.   The people of these cities are similar and congenial, and I am opposed to anything that has a tendency to divide them, or pit one against the other."

SLEEPING CAR INTERIOR ON THE WONDERLAND ROUTE.

It was to this amiable old gentleman that I owed much of the pleasure of my stay in these twin cities. He took me to see the wonderful flouring mills of Minneapolis, where I got more flour-dust on my clothes than I could have wished, and where I made little annotations in my memoranda-book, concerning the facts imparted to me by my venerable guide. He told me that St. Paul had 200,000 inhabitants, and Minneapolis 200,001 ; that Minneapolis was the largest flour market in the world, her mills having a daily aggregate

capacity of 37,450 barrels ; he said that St. Paul had seven National banks and
nine State banks, with an aggregate capital of $7,624,000 ; and that the manu-
factured products of Minneapolis for the present year would be over $84,000,000.
We had some pleasant rides together, the pleasant old pioneer and I. We
visited Fort Snelling, and looked down from its heights at the capricious river
which has made the wealth of Minneapolis. We drove to Minnehaha Falls,
quoted from the dead familiar poet, to appease his shade, drank beer within
sound of the merry little fraud which has stolen the name of the fall that Longfellow designated, and meanwhile the Judge talked to me of his son and
daughter who had gone to Tacoma.

" They are the best children in the world," my friend declared, " and you
shall carry letters to them. They have gone to make their fortunes in the city
of destiny. I never would raise my children to use the money I had given my
strength in making. It is the best way in the world to ruin a young man or
woman. I am willing to give them a start, but I want them to try their own
strength. If you do an arm up in bandages, you can not expect to be able to
use it with any execution. It is just the same with young people. I have sent
my boy out West, to the best town I could learn of, and his sister has gone along
to keep him from being homesick, and to make a home for him. I want you to
go up to the house and see them."

From what I have insinuated concerning my state of mind, it can be readily
guessed that I was not particularly desirous of an introduction to any lady. I
had come West partly to escape the sex, and was somewhat annoyed at finding
that they existed even in that part of the world which I had always thought of
as essentially a man's country. So I replied :

" I should be very glad to call at the office and see your son, Judge Curtis,
but I am not much of a society man. I am sure I should not be justified in
intruding upon your daughter."

The old gentleman was not without sensitiveness.

" Just as you please," he returned stiffly. " I will give you a note to my
son."

I took the Chicago, Milwaukee & St. Paul train to Lake Minnetonka, one
day, and rested at the Hotel St. Louis, from the fatigues consequent upon sight-
seeing. Here, amid the many islands, the gentle surprises and the wooded
banks of Minnetonka, I could reflect at ease upon these daring and dashing
young cities, which had the temerity to outdo many older and more renowned
cities in fields which those older cities had esteemed especially their own. I
took out my note-book and contemplated it in quiet, with no one to witness
my amazement.

Here was mention of one mill that has power to grind 25,000 bushels of
wheat every twenty-four hours! Its mighty belts run over its shafts at the rate
of 2,664 feet a minute! I laid back on my oars, and dizzily drew in my mind's
eye this tremendous flying and whirling, this shifting and grinding! All the

power of those twin cities came suddenly to me; I was forced to a realization of their young greatness, their probable future, and I was glad to get back to them, and to walk on their streets at night, mingling with the gay and active crowd that walks under the bright electric illuminations. I dropped into a couple of the attractive theatres, by way of getting rid of solitude, and the next day took a hasty journey from St. Paul to White Bear Lake, an exclusive little resort, where many of the finest suburban residences stand on the shores of a modest and translucent lake.

The next day I resumed my westward journey, intending to leave the main road at Winnipeg Junction, 250 miles or more from St. Paul, and then journey north over the Duluth & Manitoba Branch of the Northern Pacific. For 125 miles the road follows the great river, through fields of corn and wheat. Before these are reached, however, the suburban stretch lying between St. Paul and Minneapolis is passed. The imposing fair buildings are to be seen here, a university building, which an agreeable conductor informed me was the Hamline University, and the new shops of the Northern Pacific.

I have all my life been afraid of being bored. I was mortally fearful that now the time of distress was at hand, and that after the entertainment of a cigar had been exhausted, I should have no resources left; for I may as well own at once that I am not one of those fortunate—or fabled—mortals, whose mind to them a kingdom is.

But in a short time we neared Anoka. Now, Anoka is a nice little town of 5,000 inhabitants, engaged in the wholesome occupations of sawing trees into lumber and turning wheat into flour. She is the seat of the county whose namesake she is ; but she interested me on none of these accounts particularly. What entertained my fancy was the logging stream, bearing the spiritous name of the Rum River, at the mouth of which she stands. The idea of plenty conveyed in the rushing of that merry little stream, and the recollection of the vast concourse of plunging logs that floated down it—all of which I saw in imagination—with the loggers in the midst, singing and swearing, entertained me while I passed Big Lake and Clear Lake, pretty prairie sheets of water, and reached the shady village of St. Cloud, which, I was informed, had the advantage of Anoka in point of population by 2,000. Granite and jasper are quarried at no great distance from this town.

I was taking careless note of this village, built on its pleasant plateau, when my attention was attracted by the frantic efforts of a lady to open a window. It is one of the banes of my life that women insist on trying to open windows. Either they should go into training and accumulate sufficient strength to successfully accomplish their purpose, or else they should cure themselves of the habit. I have invariably had the misfortune to open windows for jaundiced and dyspeptic ladies, who returned me scant thanks, and did nothing but get cinders in their eyes after the window was opened. However, I did not ring for the porter as I might have done, but, inspired with the spirit of true sacrifice, opened the window for the exhausted lady, whom, to my very great surprise, I discovered to be neither jaundiced nor dyspeptic. On the contrary, she was a rosy and well-dressed young creature, with a degree of self-sufficiency in her manner, and a remarkably candid pair of eyes in her head. I addressed a few ambiguous remarks to her. She smiled at me in a way that seemed to say she understood my embarrassment, and was sorry for me, and frankly asked me to sit down. While this invitation gratified me, it also shocked me, for in the East young ladies do not ask strange young men to sit down and talk with them, on the score of an acquaintance extending over the period of ten seconds. I had read "Daisy Miller," and I must say that, though I in no way approved of that young woman, I was not averse to meeting one of her sort—which I immediately concluded my new friend to be.

"The elms and maples of St. Cloud are very beautiful," remarked Miss Dinsmore—for this, I learned, was her name. I said they were.

"Never so beautiful here, though," she went on, as if continuing her remark without interruption from me, "as in the East."

"Then you are from the East?" I inquired.

"Everyone out here is from the East," sententiously returned Miss Dinsmore, "except a few, whose parents are from the East."

"Then that is why manners are so much more cultivated than I expected to find them," I injudiciously remarked. The candid eyes opened to a somewhat embarrassing degree.

"I guess you haven't been out here very long," was all she said, but it had the effect of an accusation, and I felt like blushing. I confessed that I had not.

"Then you are not yet a good American," she said. "We out West here are proud of, and devoted to, the whole of the United States, but you of the East are only devoted to your own little particular place. You must really stay out here, and get your ideas enlarged."

A waiter, with unrivaled elocutionary powers, announced at this point that supper was ready in the dining-car, and that this was the last statement of that fact. Miss Dinsmore started with a promptitude that spoke well for her appetite, and I followed. Now, I am fastidious about my meals. Therefore, I did not look forward with pleasure to the idea of eating on board the train; but whether it was the fact that Miss Dinsmore sugared my tea, and ordered my supper, or that the linen was spotless, and the dishes so well prepared and served, I do not know, but it is certain that I ate far more than usual. In deciding just where the credit is due in this matter, my position is a delicate one; for, while I do not wish to hold back any of the praise I feel to be the right of the cuisine of the Northern Pacific, I can not well, even by insinuation, detract from the share that the lady had in my satisfaction.

While I ate my toast, and defended myself against the intellectual onslaughts of Miss Dinsmore, I looked out on the town of Sauk Rapids, near which lay beds of granite, which my vis-a-vis assured me, with triumph in her tone, was the

THE BISMARCK BRIDGE—ICE BRIDGE, 1880; STEEL BRIDGE, 1890.

equal of any of the boasted granite of New England. When we reached Little
Falls, Miss Dinsmore consented to leave the car for a few minutes to pace the
platform. I was just casting about for some theme of conversation likely to
interest this young woman, when I beheld my corduroy friend—otherwise John
Parke, huntsman and angler—bearing down upon us, laden, as usual, to the
very bulwarks with traps. He saw me at once, and unburdening himself on the
unfortunate conductors and porters, approached me with a cordiality that was
only tempered into moderation by the fact that I had a lady with me. He
had barely acknowledged the introduction, when he broke into one of his usual
rhapsodies.

"You've missed the chance of your life," he cried. "I never saw better
shooting than there is out here, west of the Mississippi. I've been out here to
Rice Lake, and up to my knees in cat-tails and rushes and wild rice, and I've
bagged some of the best ducks you ever ate."

"But," interposed Miss Dinsmore, with a certain pathetic intonation, "we
have not eaten them."

"Rest easy," said the huntsman, with a gallant salute; "you shall have some
of them, for I have brought some aboard, and they are to be cooked for me. I
had partridge and grouse, but I gave them away; and I sighted a deer, but, unfortunately, he sighted me at the same time, and our acquaintance ended then and
there. I say, Key, if you ever have occasion to put up at the Falls, be sure and go to
the 'Antlers.' Everyone who comes out this way gunning stops there, and it is
possible to have a jolly time." After this, I seemed to be shut out of the conversation for a time, for the unconscionable hunter walked away with Miss Dinsmore, showing off his handsome legs, in their dashing top-boots and skin-tight
trousers, in a way naturally discouraging to a man in commonplace trousers, the
ugliness of which were heightened by being a little bagged at the knees. As I
could not be amused, I determined to acquire knowledge, and learned that Little
Falls possessed one of the best water-powers in the United States, constructed
in 1888, and costing $250,000. This is employed for flouring-mills and factories,
and by its aid the town of Little Falls aspires to be a manufacturing center in
the not far distant future. I also learned that the Little Falls & Dakota
Division of the Northern Pacific runs south from this point. This terminates at
Morris, eighty-eight miles from Little Falls, and runs through a country distinguished for its agricultural resources, and especially for its remarkable chain
of lakes, on which I judged my corduroy friend had been exercising his privilege
of killing. Grey Eagle has a local reputation as a summer resort, as has also
Glenwood, which is situated on Lake Minnewaska, a sheet of water, so I was
informed, of considerable size and much beauty, which offers fish of many
varieties. I meant to do my duty by the country through which I was traveling,
and therefore made careful mention of all these facts in my note-book, completing my task just in time to get in my seat as the train moved westward. I found
Mr. Parke and Miss Dinsmore in active conversation, and was glad to bury

2

myself in the pages of a novel with which I had been long burdened, but which
had not before recommended itself to me.

The only time that I care to read a novel is when I am very busy, and ought
not to. When I have nothing else to do, I lose all interest in it. In the present
case, I was interested in watching the many changes that Miss Dinsmore's face
was capable of taking to itself in a few moments. I had the impertinence to
wonder where she was going, and why, and how it chanced that she was alone.
Meanwhile, the conductor sat down beside me, and talked to me about Brainerd,
which we were now rapidly approaching. I gathered from the conversation
that the car-shops of the Northern Pacific were at Brainerd, and the machine-
shops, and the boiler-shops, and a great many other places of the same sort, and
that the railroad has a sanitarium there, where my conductor was taken care of,
in a way that he praised at great length, on the occasion of a long illness. I
had just entered in my note-book the fact that Brainerd had a population of
10,000, and that she had a most satisfactory court-house and jail, erected at a
cost of $30,000, when we reached the station, and Miss Dinsmore and my corduroy
friend plunged out into the night and upon the platform.

I considered that I already had cause for feeling aggrieved, but when my
statistical young lumberman entered at this moment, I made up my mind that
the good luck which I had always firmly considered my own had deserted me.
No sooner did this painfully accurate young man perceive me, than he
advanced with outstretched hand.

" How are you, Mr. Miller?" I said, stiffly. The reply was of a different sort.

"So glad to know, Mr. Key," he exclaimed, "that you are taking a continued
interest in the resources of the country. Have been visiting a section that I
know you would have been interested in. There is a magnificent pine forest
lying up here to the north. There is enough pine in it, sir, to build fifty cities
with, and a navy of ships. I am putting it mildly, sir, upon my word I am. If
you want to see a sample of that lumber, you ought to visit Gregory Park, right
here in Brainerd, where there are ten acres of pines set aside by the town." Mr.
Miller always spoke of trees as "lumber," as you might expect a butcher to
refer to cattle as " beef."

Parke came in with Miss Dinsmore, and heard us talking. The two sat
down by us, as if they had not been rude to me, and of course I introduced
Miller. Parke looked Miller over slowly, and put the expected inquiry.

" Pardon me, sir," he said, "but are you a sportsman ? "

I smiled softly to myself, and offered Miss Dinsmore my novel. She accepted
the stupid thing with a look of gratitude, and I forgave her for the way she
had treated me. After that I did not care how many statistics I had to
listen to.

My corduroy friend was enthusiastic over what he called the " Lake Park
Region."

" Have you never heard of that remarkable chain of lakes?" he exclaimed to me, when he saw a look of ignorance in my eyes. "Mille Lac is only twenty-two miles southeast of here, and that is—"

But Miss Dinsmore interrupted him.

"I dare say you do not know how beautiful a butternut grove is," she said to me. "The trees are so generous, so beneficent, that you feel safe and comfortable as you walk under them. And of all things that I know of in the way of forests, there is nothing I more admire than one of maple. These two trees, the butternut and the maple, grow side by side, and a long beach of white gravel runs down into the green water. There are ferns and mosses and the gentian in the woods, and in the right season one can pick hundreds of strawberries there. There are cranberry marshes near, and blueberries and raspberries grow wild. One can fish there and shoot, but I do not think," and she cast a reproachful look at the corduroy man, "that any appreciative person would want to destroy anything in such a beautiful spot." Parke shook his head at this, to him, inexplicable remark, but he knew better than to openly oppose a young woman with a chin like Miss Dinsmore's.

"I've just come down from Duluth," the lumberman remarked to Miss Dinsmore, "and I assure you I have seen some beauties."

Miss Dinsmore looked shocked.

"I hope you are not referring to ladies," she said.

"Madam," returned the lumberman with dignity, "I am referring to lakes. They are scattered among the most placid and delightful meadows, and at this season these meadows are covered with gold and purple flowers."

"The golden-rod and the aster," said the lady.

"I suppose you may not be acquainted with the fact," Miller said, "that Minnesota has no less than 10,000 lakes."

"You don't say so!" excitedly cried the corduroy man.

"You are thinking what an opportunity there is for killing," cried Miss Dinsmore.

"I suppose I am to be looked upon as a sort of public executioner," protested Parke.

We had got on the subject of lakes, and we could not get away from it. Every town we stopped at was said to be in the vicinity of some lake, and I learned that in the season this part of the country was the particular resort of the sportsmen, who, though they came by the thousand, were literally swallowed up in the vastness of this solitude, and often traveled for days without meeting a companion.

Before we reached Wadena, Miss Dinsmore had retired, after playing a merry little tune for us on a zither, the case of which had attracted my attention. We three men went out on the platform. A rolling plain lay stretched out beyond us, broken with gentle groves. The little place seemed to have an abundance of activities. Two grain elevators loomed up black in the starlight. I heard from a drummer that there were six hotels in the place, a flouring-mill, with a

MONTANA HORSE RANCH.

(20)

capacity for 100 barrels a day, a foundry, and a large trade with the surrounding grain country.

The drummer had just come from the Black Hills Branch of the Northern Pacific. This runs west from Wadena. He, too, was talking about lakes, and aroused the enthusiasm of the corduroy man to such an extent that he had an extra " lay-over " marked on his ticket, and left us to test the delights of Battle Lake—or rather the two Battle Lakes, famous for their beauty of dell and cove and shore, but more famous still for their marvelous variety of fish. We traveled a few miles together before the proper station was reached, Parke meanwhile gathering up his endless quantity of traps, and turning one enraptured ear to the recital of the tales of wonderful catches that the commercial gentleman poured into it. I, unfortunately, made no note of these tales, and can not reproduce them. To a man who knows nothing about fishing, and who has never read Izaak Walton since his early youth, these stories naturally have little point. I was more interested in the description of a chain of lakes much sought by the canoeist, and having easy portage between them. I peered out of the window into the darkness, wondering how far distant was that melancholy ground on which the Indians of the Sioux and Chippewa Nations poured out their fierce and hereditary hatred in such unavailing strife.

The instructive drummer spoke of Fergus Falls and Wahpeton, on the Fergus & Black Hills Branch, as being good towns to do business in, both now rejoicing in elevators, the inevitable court-house, opera-house, and factories and mills.

Detroit was the next point passed which offered particular attractions to me. This is becoming a very popular summer resort, having a hotel of gay architecture, suggesting midsummer pleasures, situated on Detroit Lake, a crescent-shaped sheet of water, with alternate banks and beaches. The lake has attractions of the sort likely to allure my corduroy friend, but it is sought especially as a place of refuge from the heat of the East in the months of July and August. The town itself is in a bower of trees, and forests flank it.

At Winnipeg Junction I bade good-bye to my friends with a certain regret —not because I was fond of them. I did not consider it good form to be fond of anyone on such short acquaintance. Impulsiveness is a characteristic of the Wild West. In the East we temper our enthusiasm with discretion.

I arrived in Winnipeg the next day, having enjoyed all the conveniences of a Pullman sleeper and dining-car by the way. Winnipeg is a town which quaintly combines the enterprise of the present with the relics of an interesting past. The Hudson Bay Company (vaguely associated in my mind with dashing French voyageurs, with the Indian at the best of his alertness, subtlety, and daring, and with fur-hung halls where the nights of rare reunions were spent in memorable carousals) has here a most important post, and it still represents a wealth and power which has only ceased to seem extraordinary because the mind has become accustomed to the idea of great commercial organizations.

Winnipeg has a population of 25,000, at which I might have been surprised had I not learned the extent of her trade relations, which extend through the Canadian possessions as far west as the Rocky Mountains.

Three days later, having transacted my business, I took the train for the South, first by the Northern Pacific & Manitoba road, and then by the Duluth & Manitoba Division of the Northern Pacific.

It was one of those clear, bright days, with a brisk wind, so common in that climate, and the world looked especially clean and well cared for, as I went rushing southward. Pembina is the oldest town in the whole West, having been settled in 1801, by the colonists brought to this country by the Earl of Selkirk. The population is peculiar. Canadians, French-Canadians, Icelanders, and Americans make up the little town, which, in ceasing to be a mere trading-post, has become the market for the rich farming country round about. The valley of the Red River of the North has a fame for hard spring wheat which had reached even my ears—who am the most ignorant of men on such subjects. And I now learned that the yield was seldom below twenty bushels an acre, and often over thirty. Grafton is another town whose prosperity is owing to the rich agricultural country in its vicinity, and Grand Forks, which has a population of 10,000, shares the same advantage, and adds to it an active industry in logging. Red Lake Falls stands at the junction of Clearwater and Red Lake rivers, which, between them, have no less than thirteen water-powers.

I found myself not averse to getting back to Winnipeg Junction, for I had a hope that I might meet some of my old acquaintances. I was beginning to lose my dread of the statistical lumberman, and to forgive the corduroy man for suspecting me of an inclination to kill, and I never did lay up her sex against Miss Dinsmore. That young lady was to stop off with friends for a few days, somewhere, and the lumberman being on a tour for the express accumulation of knowledge, and the sportsman being the creature of caprice, I was likely, if my luck did not desert me, to meet any or all of them at any time.

Business done, I was ready to devote myself to pleasure—or the nearest approach to it that I could hope to find. So I settled down to a quiet enjoyment of the days, caring little what turned up next. I had a consciousness that I would sleep in a well-made bed, have well-cooked meals, carefully served, and the privilege of lolling all day in softly upholstered seats, and looking out upon an ever-changing scene. The prospect was comfortable. I was lazy—out of love with the world, and in love, just at present, with idleness. I did not imagine that the West held any personal interest for me, but I did not object to looking at it—it is as well to encourage these young and struggling communities. So, with a silk dust-cap on my head, my feet comfortably encased in patent-leather ties, a pile of novels by my side, a box of cigars always in easy reach in the dining-car, I settled down to my journey, and wondered how long it took a New York woman to forget a man she had driven to despair; but the most humiliating part of it was, that in spite of all attempts to summon up sentiment on the subject, I was disgustingly comfortable in spite of the despair. Whether it was the cooking, or the scenery, or the natural revolt of the mind too long troubled, I do not know; but the fact remains, I was comfortable.

Figures do not mean very much to me, and the facts that I heard adduced by the many statisticians that I seemed fated to meet did not make the impression they were expected to. As I left Minnesota, and entered upon the prairie stretches of Dakota, I was entertained by the sight, entirely new to me. Here were the plains, but a few years ago the haunt of the Indian and buffalo! Now, the wheat of North Dakota has the reputation of being the best in the world, and when one remembers how recently it acquired this reputation, and compares the population of the State at present with that of five years ago, he is persuaded that no country contains more surprises than these United States.

In this section of the country, a yield of twenty bushels per acre is usual, and twenty-five bushels is not surprising. The flour produced from hard spring wheat is said to be an especially valuable commodity, bakers being able to get 250 pounds of bread from a barrel of flour made from the spring wheat, and only 225 pounds from the same quantity of flour ground from winter wheat. At Fargo I made a note, in my fast-filling memoranda-book, to the effect that the Northern Pacific sends out a branch road, called the Fargo & South-Western Branch of the Northern Pacific Railroad, which extends to Lisbon and La Moure, both thriving towns in the midst of a good agricultural country. At Edgeley, the western terminus of this line, it is possible to make connections with the Milwaukee road, and at Oakes, the terminus of a southern extension, with the Chicago & North-Western.

Having communicated these facts to my invaluable book, I was delighted to see, approaching down the length of the car, Miss Dinsmore, accompanied by two elderly and discreet ladies. With a friendliness I thought very flattering, Miss Dinsmore took a seat adjoining mine, and introduced the two discreet ladies as her aunts. Then she helped them remove their brown veils, which were exactly alike, as were all their clothes. The ladies were not well seated before I met with another surprise in the appearance on the scene of the familiar figures of the lumberman and the gentleman in corduroy. I was naturally surprised at seeing all of my old friends appear together, but I thought it would be rude to ask questions, and contented myself with beginning a conversation such as I hoped would meet with the approval of the elderly ladies.

"A beautiful country," said I, affably.

"'Tis, for them that appreciates it," said one of the ladies, who was evidently more decisive than grammatical.

"I'm sure I appreciate it," I said in an injured tone.

"Well," said the decisive aunt, "you look as if you had sense."

Miss Dinsmore smiled at me. I have always heard that women who have not fine teeth laugh with their eyes; but the young lady opposite had certainly no occasion for concealing her teeth. I was afraid, in spite of Miss Dinsmore's

YELLOWSTONE RIVER AND CRAZY MOUNTAINS

presence, that the society was going to be depressing, when suddenly one of the aunts, who apparently had a desire to be hospitable, opened a small basket, and offered a portion of its contents to me.

"Better take a doughnut," said she, sociably. "You are likely to get hungry fifty times a day on the cars." I refused with some embarrassment, and Miss Dinsmore came to the rescue.

"There is no need for fretting about hunger in this land," she said. "Fargo, you know, is the headquarters of the Northern Pacific Elevator Company, and I hear they have fifty elevators round about here. I have been out visiting the Dalrymple farm. I suppose you do not know what that signifies, Mr. Key. There are twenty square miles of wheat there—I never felt so proud of my country as when I saw that wheat-field. You can not imagine how yellow that wheat was, or how responsive to the wind. When the sun and shadow played over it there was not *one* shade of yellow, but a hundred. It is the very embodiment of plenty! And in harvest-time twenty-four self-binding reapers are driven over the fields at a time, cutting, so I have heard, at one sweep a swath of 192 feet."

My two friends, the lumberman and the sportsman, did not seem interested in this conversation. In fact, they appeared to unite in taking a very serious view of life. I discovered Parke darting vicious side-long glances at the discreet and elderly aunts. The ladies moved to the other side of the car to enjoy something of peculiar interest in the landscape, and I went over to where these dejected fellow-travelers were sitting.

"What are you doing in this country?" I asked. "There are no trees to measure and nothing to kill, unless it is prairie dogs."

They both looked at me and said not a word. I purchased a cigar and discreetly withdrew. Meanwhile the train went whizzing on through the beautiful Valley City in its amphitheatre of hills; through Sanborn, where a branch of the road runs north through a rich wheat country to Cooperstown, and on to Jamestown.

Substantial and pleasant is Jamestown with its compact brick blocks, its wide streets, and its enterprise. The gentleman in corduroy recovered his spirits sufficiently to tell me that the Jamestown & Northern Railway ran from here up to Devil's Lake, in which he assured me it was possible to catch fish of the most remarkable size and quality.

"And if you want to shoot geese, you can't go to a better place for it," he added; but he said it sadly, and it was evident that a blight had fallen upon his once exuberant spirits.

We were pulling into the Coteaux de Missouri, that remarkable table-land which, like most glacial deposits, offers rich opportunities to the agriculturist. It lies between the valleys of the James and Missouri rivers, and runs north into the British possessions.

As we passed Steele, Miss Dinsmore came over to say that the introduction of trees not indigenous to the soil was succeeding very well in North Dakota, and that box-elder, cotton-wood, and willow were being raised in a large nursery in the vicinity. It was strange for a woman to be so exact in her information, and I remarked as much to her. She said she had an interest in the country at large, and had read up on Dakota. But I saw there was something behind this, for the two gentlemen looked darker than ever. But, nothing daunted, Miss Dinsmore discoursed to me on the wonderful richness of the sage-brush land. To a man raised in the East, a stretch of sage-brush has a most discouraging appearance. It seems like a curse and a blight. But I soon became convinced that when once the sage-brush is removed, it is the richest farming country in the world.

"Dakota does not seem to have many rivers," I said to Miss Dinsmore, to test her information on the subject. She was up in arms in a minute—quite as if I had been depreciating a piece of personal property.

"I am surprised to hear you," she cried. "Beside the Missouri and the Red River, which are navigable, there are the Cannon Ball, and the Heart, the Sweet Briar, and the Little Missouri. And, speaking of water, the Dakotas have the most remarkable system of artesian wells known in the world. The range of present wells east and west is fully fifty miles, while north and south it follows from Yankton, on the Missouri River, to Jamestown, here on the Northern Pacific Railroad. The James River Valley is the center of the water belt. There are also two other areas of subterranean water partially exploited, and they are both in North Dakota. In addition to the rivers and the wells, the Dakotas have a large area covered with small lakes and lagoons. So you see, Mr. Key, there will be no lack of water here."

"Good thing," said I, "seeing what the prohibition tendencies are."

We passed through Bismarck, the capital of North Dakota, a healthy town with a reputation which needs no confirmation from me. Miss Dinsmore whispered that there was coal in the region of which there were good reports. She warned me that I should miss much if I stayed in the car, for we were about to cross the Missouri on one of the finest bridges in the western country. Therefore, against all rules, we stood on the platform and craned our necks over to view with admiration this wonderful structure of trusses, piers, girders, and cords of steel and iron. The Missouri, yellow and strong, flowed southward.

"It is a little pathetic," said Miss Dinsmore, who was leaning over the brass bar in the vestibule of the car, "to look up this Missouri Valley and think of the change that has come to it. The Indian has gone, and the buffalo; and the bear and the beaver are all but gone. We turned the corn-fields of the Indian into battle-grounds. Civilization must go on, I suppose, but it is rather hard that the Indian must always be the victim of it."

We arrived at the village of Mandan, and, getting off at the station, wandered into an excellent curio shop that invites the promenader from the platform. The owl and the eagle, the American lion and the grizzly, are all here. There

were some specimens of exquisitely decorated pottery here, also, which
had been dug from bluffs two miles from Mandan, at the junction of the
Hart and Missouri rivers. Here are the remains of a mysterious people for
whom the students have not yet been able to account. They show a knowledge
of art which certainly was not possessed by the American Indians as we have
know them. The cemetery of this gigantic race covers about 100 acres, and
will furnish interesting study for some American Schlieman.

I must not forget to mention that Fort Abraham Lincoln lies five miles
southwest of Mandan.

Just beyond Gladstone lies Dickinson, which, with its brick manufacturing,
its sandstone and coal-beds, lies in the midst of a country well adapted to agriculture and grazing.

It chanced to be nearing twilight as we came into the Bad Lands; these are
more popularly called Pyramid Park, but I cling, myself, to the name given
them by the old French voyageurs.

A gentleman of universal information pointed out varieties of lignite, argil-
laceous limestone, friable sandstone, and potsherd, and gave me a dissertation
on the Pliocene Age, and the effects of fire and water; but I saw the place with
different eyes. To me it was a blasted heath, on which Macbeth's witches
might have met; or a spot that might appropriately be selected by the witches in
which to celebrate Walpurgis night. Buttes of brown, of gray and white with
tops of red and cuts of dull, sulphurous blue, twisted and rent, and distorted
into shapes so tortuous that to my mind they suggested only suffering and strife,
stretched out before the eye everywhere. My friends told me that the land was
not unwholesome—that even on the top of these stricken-looking hills, rich grains
and vegetables would grow; but the dance of the witches was all I could see,
and I was sure I should never seek to dwell among such scenes, unless, in some
hour of deeper depression than I had ever experienced, I should find a subtle
sympathy amid these grotesque and unique scenes.

At this time I noticed that a strange quiet was falling upon our party. The
discreet maiden aunts no longer helped themselves to waters from their wicker
baskets. Though Miss Dinsmore's cheeks were red, and her eyes were unusually
bright, she had ceased to converse; and as for the two gentlemen, their gloom
had deepened until, as Charles Lamb has put it, "they might have thrown a
damper over a funeral."

We had just reached a little town which intruded its calm commonplaceness
into this astounding scene, when Miss Dinsmore volunteered the information
that she should leave us at the next station. I expressed my dismay with a
gesture.

"Yes," said Miss Dinsmore; "I am going to live back here in the country
about fifty miles." I regarded her in horrified astonishment. She colored, but
it was evidently not from resentment.

"You see," explained Miss Dinsmore, "I stopped at Fargo to get my aunts,

GEYSERS AND FALLS IN THE YELLOWSTONE NATIONAL PARK.

who have come on to attend my wedding." That explained everything—the depression of the lumberman and the corduroy man, and the subdued mood that had fallen on the party.

"I am delighted to hear it," I cried. "I presume that you know where you will find anyone in this country to marry, but I can see nothing but blasted rocks and barren valley."

"Then I will tell you what you shall do," Miss Dinsmore cried; "you shall come to my wedding, and I will show you miles of fertile valley behind these rocks where your witches dance, and instead of its being a spot selected by Mephistopheles from which to curse the world, you will find plenty and comfort, and, what will doubtless surprise you more, companies of good jolly fellows who make the best of friends."

Then she dilated upon the great cattle ranches, and the home-like "shacks" where the ranchmen live. After this, it was not hard to guess that it was with one of these ranchmen, and in one of these "shacks," that Miss Dinsmore expected to find consolation for living in such a country.

We left the road at Mingusville, and I was pleased to find that the lumberman and the gentleman in corduroy were to accompany us; but it being already the "edge of evening," as Lowell puts it, and the road being tortuous in the extreme, it was thought best for us all to wait over night at an inn. The gentleman to whom Miss Dinsmore had paid the compliment of coming across the Dakota plains to meet, joined us. He was an enormous young fellow, with a black, drooping mustache, slightly faded by the sun, who, in spite of the fact that he had come to meet his bride, wore a gray flannel shirt, knotted at the throat with a silk handkerchief of the most uncompromising tints. He was so full of life and activity that I was in constant fear that he might break some of the furniture, or tread upon my toes—an offense which I never forgive—or accidentally sit upon one of the prim maiden aunts and demolish her. I have never yet met a young man of whom there seemed to be so much. It was not his size alone; it was what in Boston they would call his "atmosphere."

The next morning, mounted on a number of the capricious cayuses, we started on our journey. The sun was still low in the east, red and large, and phantasmal mists were wreathing about all these uncanny hills and hollows. I felt as if I were riding through the land where the German gnomes dwelt, and would not have been surprised at any moment to see a troop of them, humpbacked and hideous, working with their anvils in this infernal forge, where the scoria of dead fires strewed the ground, and in some hollows of which mines of lignite were burning, as they had been ever since the memory of man—a sort of eternal adoration to the unwholesome spirit of the place. A few gnarled, twisted trees, which seemed to be protesting against their lives, grew by the water-courses, and all over the country grew the short bunch-grass, which, when it is cured, is said to make nutritious hay; and side by side with it grew the sage-brush, the color of the mistletoe. Brown, bare, and bizarre, the

landscape stood for the very incarnation of desolation and *grotesquerie*. The
cattle roam in great herds over " round-ups " of fifty miles or more, feeding on
the fine prairies back of the buttes, in the summer, and in the winter taking
refuge among the buttes and in the sparsely timbered sections.

It was two days before I left the hospitable shack of my friend, the ranch-
man. I need not tell all I saw in this remarkable country, but I was convinced
that it was possible for a man to make a fortune there if he understood cattle-
raising. A wild, adventurous, not unfascinating life it is, with a rich promise
of opulence to aid the patience and assist the judgment. As for the interior
of the shack, it was one of the most delightful I ever saw. The floors were
covered with beautiful skins, the walls decorated with antlers, and cabinets of
the exquisite crystals and agates chipped from the buttes of Pyramid Park;
the great fire-place was made of squares of the red potsherd, cemented together;
three or four hammocks hung about the room; a buffet, not innocent of select
cordials and liquors, some fowling-pieces, and a guitar, made up an *ensemble*
which could not but be inviting. I was relieved, too, to find that my little friend
would not be without woman's society here. Many of the ranchmen have their
wives with them, and it goes without saying that where is money there will be
gaiety.

Bidding farewell to our friends, including the discreet maiden aunts, I and
my two traveling companions returned by the same weird road over which we
had previously journeyed, and took a train bound for the setting sun. For 340
miles we followed the windings of the Yellowstone, a river so clear and bright,
so full of bewitching cascades and green islands, that it seemed each hour as if
it had been freshly born and had no relation with this old and weary world.

We passed the lively town of Glendive, and then several quiet and wholesome
hamlets, at last reaching Miles City, a town which has the distinction of being
the only one, save Bozeman, on the Northern Pacific lines which did not owe its
origin to the building of the road. It is at present the key to a rich cattle
country, there being 700,000 cattle on the ranges round about. Ninety miles
farther on, after passing through a historic tract of country, made famous with
the names of some of our best Indian fighters, we came to Custer, the station
for Fort Custer, which lies thirty miles distant, and, while not equaling Fort
Keough, which lies just beyond Miles City, in its equipment or garrison, is
one of the most notable military posts in the West. It was near here that the
yellow-haired hero whose name the fort bears met with his memorable and
tragic death.

Billings is a town of steady growth, situated at the foot of Clark's Fork
Bottom, in the midst of characteristic Western scenery, at once picturesque and
peculiar. It is only second to Miles City as a shipping-point for cattle;
and gold, silver, and coal are found in the country tributary. The coal comes
from Red Lodge, and the gold and silver mines are adjacent to Cooke City,
and are reached by the Yellowstone Branch of the Northern Pacific Railroad in

connection with a wagon-road from Cinnabar. The gentleman in corduroy deserted us at this point, being won by tales of wild hunting adventures in this country, and by the promise of marvelous scenery. "I will see you again," he said, as we parted. "I am sure it is our fate to meet. I would go on with you, but there is a cañon south of here that men should be willing to travel a thousand miles to see, and I am too patriotic to turn my back on it."

At Big Timber, my lumberman deserted me, and I was obliged to go on my journey alone. He also paid me the compliment of saying that he parted from me with regret; and, while he could urge no cañon in excuse of this disloyalty, he thought the flourishing saw-mill a sufficient excuse for leaving any man, even his best friend. I used to tell him that if he ever got to Heaven, and found the gates were really of jasper, he would refuse to go in. That man had no sympathy with anything but hardwood.

At Springdale we took on a number of persons who had been recuperating at Hunter's Hot Springs, and at Livingston—of which I will say more at another time—we left the comfortable seclusion of our Pullman car for a train less exclusive though equally luxurious, running south to Cinnabar, the gateway of the Yellowstone National Park.

I hardly know how to describe the ride from Livingston to Cinnabar. The road lies through the third or lower cañon of the Yellowstone, which is an ancient lake-bed, and bears the name of Paradise Valley. Through it the river tumbles and pounds and laughs, clear as crystal and cold as ice. The rich ranches, stretching beyond the level up onto the moraines, look like great Persian rugs with their harmonious blending of colors. On each side the mountains rise, each bearing its grim history of volcanic struggles, of glacial epochs. On Cinnabar Mountain the strata is vertical, and in one remarkable spot, where the stratum of soft material is washed out, there is a formidable slide 2,000 feet in length between jagged walls of rock. But this is not a district in which one wishes to specify and particularize. I, and I am sure many others, will prefer to take it as a beautiful whole. At Cinnabar, coaches were in waiting to take us to the Mammoth Hot Springs Hotel, and we drove down through a rugged and majestic country to this capacious hostelry. There the evening was made memorable to me by three things—some excellent music, which I believe is provided every night of the summer for guests, the making of some pleasant new acquaintances, and the reading of that portion of Talmage's sermon, written after his visit to the West, in which he refers to the scenery of the Yellowstone Park. It was read to us by a young lady from New Orleans, with the dulcet inflections for which the ladies of her city are noted:

"But the most wonderful part of this American Continent is the Yellowstone Park. My visit there made upon me an impression that will last forever. After all poetry has exhausted itself, and all the Morans and Bierstadts and the other enchanting artists have completed their canvas, there will be other revelations to make, and other stories of its beauty and wrath, splendor and agony, to be recited. The Yellowstone Park is a geologist's paradise. In

PHARAOH—HOODOO COUNTRY, YELLOWSTONE PARK

some portions of it there seems to be the anarchy of the elements fire and water, and the vapor born of that marriage terrific. Geyser cones or hills of crystal that have been over 5,000 years growing. In places, the earth throbbing, sobbing, groaning, quaking with aqueous paroxysm.

"At the expiration of every sixty-five minutes, one of the geysers tosses its boiling water 185 feet in the air, and then descends into swinging rainbows. Caverns of pictured walls large enough for the sepulcher of the human race. Formations of stone in shape and color of calla lily, of heliotrope, of rose, of cowslip, of sunflower, and of gladiola. Sulphur and arsenic, and oxide of iron, with their delicate pencils, turning the hills into a Luxemburg or a Vatican picture gallery. The so-called Thanatopsis Geyser, exquisite as the Bryant poem it was named after, and the so-called Evangeline Geyser, lovely as the Longfellow heroine it commemorates. The so-called Pulpit Terrace, from its white elevation, preaching mightier sermons of God than human lips ever uttered. The so-called Bethesda Geyser, by the warmth of which invalids have already been cured, the Angel of Health continually stirring the waters. Enraged craters, with heat at 500 degrees only a little below the surface.

"Wide reaches of stone of intermingled colors—blue as the sky, green as the foliage, crimson as the dahlia, white as the snow, spotted as the leopard, tawny as the lion, grizzly as the bear—in circles, in angles, in stars, in coronets, in stalactites, in stalagmites. Here and there are petrified growths, or the dead trees and vegetation of other ages kept through a process of natural embalmment. In some places, waters as innocent and smiling as a child making a first attempt to walk from its mother's lap, and not far off as foaming and frenzied and ungovernable as a maniac in murderous struggle with his keepers.

"But after you have wandered along the geyserite enchantment for days, and begin to feel that there can be nothing more of interest to see, you suddenly come upon the peroration of all majesty and grandeur—the Grand Cañon. It is here that, it seems to me—and I speak it with reverence—Jehovah seems to have surpassed himself. It seems a great gulch let down into the eternities. Here, hung up and let down, and spread abroad, are all the colors of land and sea and sky; upholstering of the Lord God Almighty; best work of the Architect of worlds; sculpturing by the Infinite; masonry by an Omnipotent trowel. Yellow ! You never saw yellow unless you saw it there. Red ! You never saw red unless you saw it there. Violet ! You never saw violet unless you saw it there. Triumphant banners of color. In a cathedral of basalt, Sunrise and Sunset married by the setting of rainbow ring.

"Gothic arches, Corinthian capitals, and Egyptian basilicas built before human architecture was born; huge fortifications of granite constructed before war forged its first cannon; Gibraltars and Sebastopols that never can be taken; Alhambras, where kings of strength and queens of beauty reigned long before the first earthly crown was empearled; thrones on which no one but the King of heaven and earth ever sat; fount of waters at which the lesser hills are baptized, while the giant cliffs stand round as sponsors. For thousands of years before that scene was unveiled to human sight, the elements were busy, and the geysers were hewing away with their hot chisels, and glaciers were pounding with their cold hammers, and hurricanes were cleaving with their lightning strokes, and hailstones giving the finishing touches, and after all these forces of Nature had done their best, in our century the curtain dropped, and the world had a new and divinely inspired revelation, the Old Testament written on papyrus, the New Testament written on parchment, and now this last testament written on the rocks.

3

" Hanging over one of the cliffs, I looked off until I could not get my breath, then, retreating to a less exposed place, I looked down again. Down there is a pillar of rock that in certain conditions of the atmosphere looks like a pillar of blood. Yonder are fifty feet of emerald on a base of 500 feet of opal; walls of chalk resting on pedestals of beryl; turrets of light tumbling on floors of darkness; the brown brightening into golden; snow of crystal melting into fire of carbuncle; flaming red cooling into russet; cold blue warming into saffron; dull gray kindling into solferino; morning twilight flushing midnight shadows; auroras crouching among rocks.

" Yonder is an eagle's nest on a shaft of basalt. Through an eye-glass we see among it the young eagles, but the stoutest arm of our group can not hurl a stone near enough to disturb the feathered domesticity. Yonder are heights that would be chilled with horror but for the warm robe of forest foliage with which they are enwrapped; altars of worship at which nations might kneel; domes of chalcedony on temples of porphyry. See all this carnage of color up and down the cliffs; it must have been the battle-field of the war of the elements. Here are all the colors of the wall of heaven, neither the sapphire nor the chrysolite, nor the topaz, nor the jacinth, nor the amethyst, nor the jasper, nor the twelve gates of twelve pearls wanting. If spirits, bound from earth to heaven, could pass up by way of this cañon, the dash of heavenly beauty would not be so overpowering. It would only be from glory to glory. Ascent through such earthly scenery, in which the crystal is so bright and the red so flaming, would be fit preparation for the ' sea of glass mingled with fire.'

" Standing there in the Grand Cañon of the Yellowstone Park on the morning of August 9th, for the most part we held our peace, but after a while it flashed upon me with such power I could not help but say to my comrades : ' What a hall this would be for the last judgment ! ' See that mighty cascade with the rainbows at the foot of it ! If those waters congealed and transfixed with the agitations of that day, what a place they would make for the shining feet of a judge of quick and dead! And those rainbows look now like the crowns to be cast at his feet. At the bottom of this great cañon is a floor, on which the nations of the earth might stand, and all up and down these galleries of rock the nations of heaven might sit. And what reverberation of archangels' trumpets there would be through all these gorges, and from all these caverns, and over all these heights ! Why should not the greatest of all the days the world shall ever see close amid the grandest scenery Omnipotence ever built ? "

After this it seems superfluous for me to mention anything I saw or thought in this wonderful country; but it is pleasant to write the assurance that not only will the visitor of the future see all that has been described by this most graphic of preachers, but he will also be able to visit the Yellowstone Lake, where hotels are now completed, and the steel-hulled boat, capable of accommodating 150 persons, is ready for use.

I left the Park with a feeling of physical vigor, but of mental fatigue. I had seen and felt too much. The excitement and exaltation had been too great, and I was glad to get among more commonplace scenes.

Of the many friends I had met in the Park, only the gentleman who bore the descriptive name of Mr. Bolter was to accompany me on my westward journey. He confided to me the fact that having spent two fortunes in traveling, he was now preparing to make a third, and was consequently in search of investments which would bring him quick returns. In these investments I afterward became much interested, and indeed the interest began at Livingston. Mr. Bolter decided that, as Livingston was the central headquarters of an important railroad division and the junction point of the Park branch with the main line, it was bound to grow, aside from the fact that it is, and ever must be, the chief town in an important mining country, embracing such well-known camps as Cooke City, Castle Mountain, and Neihart. The demand for houses and the astonishing prices cheerfully paid for rent induced my speculative friend to purchase ground and order the erection of several substantial dwellings. As these residences were bespoken, to use the words of Mr. Bolter, even before the contract for their erection was completed, he started westward in the best of moods, and insisted on treating me at each meal to an economical bottle of Zinfandel. It was during these times that we gravely discussed the golden State of Montana and its future. I learned that the rivers in the State were navigated by steamboats a distance of 1,500 miles. I learned of the rich valleys by the large rivers; of the great growth of trees in the northwestern part of the State; of the vast ranges of cattle and sheep; of the sweet and nutritious grasses, and, above all and over all, the fabulous tales of mineral wealth.

As I write I observe in my note-book a little pasted clipping cut from an interview with Col. R. J. Hinton, Engineer to the Senate Committee on Irrigation. It is as follows :

" On the east side of the continental ranges, the abundant waters that supply and make up the Missouri and Mississippi all take up their rise and flow through Montana. There is enough water in them to easily reclaim 40,000,000 acres of fertile land, now entirely idle. The stream beds flow from 250 to 500 feet below the surface of the great table-lands. There are large valley areas also, but these areas will never prove as good farming land as that of the plains above. Good engineering, however, will be required to so impound the waters of these streams as to enable them to be turned from their beds for the irrigation of the table-lands. In Montana at the present moment only about 650,000 acres are under cultivation by irrigation. Bozeman is the center of the largest irrigated grain section. Missoula, in the extreme northwest portion of the State, promises to be the best orchard and small grain region."

With the promise of such wealth as this, I said to myself, added to the natural wealth that already exists in these brown and rugged mountains, what may not the State of Montana become! At Bozeman, a beautiful little city of 4,500 people, I learned that I was at the very gateway of Gallatin Valley, so noted for its wheat, its oats, and its barley. The Gallatin Valley, I remembered, was considered by the Senatorial Committee on Irrigation as one of the most salient examples of the good that could be worked by irrigation.

Near Bozeman are also rich coal-fields. These lie in close proximity to the town, and are of pure bituminous coal, excellently adapted for coking purposes, and being therefore available for the smelters. Bozeman is fortunate in its educational advantages, having, in addition to its public schools, a Presbyterian academy.

CONCLAVE OF THE HOODOOS.—HOODOO COUNTRY, YELLOWSTONE PARK.

Near Gallatin, where the Madison, Gallatin, and Jefferson rivers unite with such equal and mighty force that the first explorers could not tell which of them deserved to be called the continuation of the Missouri, I saw the new branch road of the Northern Pacific, running south and west to Butte, and bringing that city 120 miles nearer St. Paul. The next two weeks were spent by my speculative friend and myself in a country which can never fail to impress itself on my imagination.

These days are so full of interest that I hardly know which to speak of first. There was the day at Townsend, for instance. Townsend is in itself a quiet little place, more interesting to the tourist for the reason that it sends a daily stage to White Sulphur Springs than for any other reason; but not far from Townsend, across the Missouri Valley, in a northwesterly direction, is a wonderful series of precipitous cañons among the mountains. Cut and wrenched by the elements and fantastically colored, polished with avalanches and beautified with mists, Hellgate Cañon presents the most awful beauty that can be found in the State of Montana. To tell the truth, for the most part the mountains are not impressive around Helena and Butte; they are generous swelling hills, mighty in size, but not impressive to the eye, and when not covered with snow are clothed with the russet-colored grasses.

We reached Helena on a September day, and the picture that we saw was a brown one. Everywhere the generous hills rose up to the sky, covered with that uniform brown tint; the very buildings themselves seemed to tone in with the prevailing color; the sky made the only variation. Stretching out beyond the city lay the fertile Prickly Pear Valley, and up and down the slopes of the streets climbed the houses built on ground that has become more valuable than the gold that used to be washed from those same streets in the days of the rich placer mining.

My friend and I registered at the Broadwater Hotel. The Broadwater, which is located on the Northern Pacific Railroad, near the city, is one of the most remarkable hotels at which it was ever my privilege to stop. It cost, so I was assured, and as I can easily believe, $350,000; but this includes a pleasant park, whose greenery is most grateful to the eye wearied of that brown landscape. And it also has a sanitarium at which the people of Helena find no little part of their amusement. A steam street motor runs from Helena to the Broadwater, which lies about three miles distant from the city, and passes through the imposing residence portion in which stand the homes of many millionaire miners.

The occasion for the building of the sanitarium in this green glen is the existence of the Hot Springs, which contain chemicals said to be especially desirable for a person suffering with the rheumatism. I did not suffer with the rheumatism, but I was quite willing to enter the sanitarium, whose Moorish architecture at once attracted and puzzled my eye. Once within, I stood astonished. A tank, 300 feet long and 180 feet wide, of clear, steaming water flowed

before me. Above was a roof of arched and polished pine; around, a glimmer
of prismatic colors, for the sides of the building are of glass of the most
brilliant tints. At one end of the tank, over a great pile of straggling rocks,
flows a small cataract of green water; and oriole windows, set with stained glass,
are so arranged that, in whatever position the sun chances to be, a rainbow is
sure to play in this musical, swift-flowing fall. But this was not all that interested me. All about this pile of rocks, right in the clear rush of water, stood
groups of nymphs—nymphs, it is true, in very modern bathing-suits. Their
attitudes were none the less graceful from the fact that they were not free from
self-consciousness; and all the while the air was rent with the playful shrieks of
several hundred more nymphs who disported in the tank below. With tumbled,
dripping hair and flourish of white arms, and struggling and gurgling as some
inexpert swimmer went beyond her distance in the tank, with fights in which
Neptune and Aphrodite might have taken part, and the ever-changing transformation up there in the falls where the prettiest of the nymphs posed, an hour
passed very rapidly.

The hotel itself is furnished in exquisite taste, with cool, inviting bath-rooms
among its luxuries, and a table service as dainty and complete as anything one
could find in the most luxurious home. Sitting here in the pleasant office I
fell in with a gentleman who, in the phraseology of the country, had recently
" struck it rich."

This man's history was a tragic one. His manners were convincing, being a
reminiscence of the time when it was dangerous to question the accuracy of a
Montana citizen. He was the most hospitable and friendly of men to his
friends, but to his enemies—but I mistake. He had no enemies. They were
all dead. Fortunately for my health, we were friends, and he used to smoke
my cigars with child-like confidence.

" I've been a trail-blazer in my day," he vouchsafed, " an' there aint no man
in this country knows more 'bout the place than me."

This honest pride was justified by the facts he confided to me and my note-
book, some of which I reproduce, seeing in my mind's eye, as I do so, this good
man with his hard hands, his keen eyes, his checked suit, diamonds, and high-
heeled boots.

From him I learned that Helena, standing, as she does, midway between
Tacoma and St. Paul, has a signal advantage commercially. She boasts a population of 22,000, an increase of 10,000 in three years. She is the capital of the
proud young State, and is likely to remain so. Until 1892 this honor is assured
her by her charter. In her First National Bank alone she has a deposit of
$4,000,000. And this is a fair indication of the immense wealth invested in the
mines, smelters, flumes, and cattle ranches round about. Her two reduction
works each have a capacity of fifty tons daily. Millions of dollars have been
expended in her great smelter. Business blocks and residences of pretension
and a solidity, too, seldom met with in America, are being raised in every

direction. This is the result of no unhealthy "boom," but comes from a sort of concerted action on the part of Helena citizens. For many years, now, fortunes have been a-making at Helena, and the people have a reckless way of referring to millions where the more discreet easterner would speak of thousands. But only recently has the rich man of Helena come to appreciate the significance of his money. In short, the people of Helena have passed the first stage of wealth, and reached the second. They have made their money; they are now beginning to spend it.

There are five public schools in Helena, employing at least thirty teachers. The Montana Wesleyan University is being erected five miles from Helena. It will be reached by a motor, and is situated in the midst of 200 acres of rich valley land. The cost of the building will be $50,000. At Bozeman there is also a Presbyterian academy, in the midst of those placid and luxuriant gardens which distinguish that town from those surrounding it, and prove that flower and garden-culture in Montana is only a matter of successful irrigation. At Deer Lodge there is a large Presbyterian college which has grown till it occupies three imposing buildings. But the facts on which my mining friend most prided himself were those which referred to the material wealth of the young State. He assured me that at the last assessment the valuation of assessable property in fourteen counties was $60,666,924.70. The output of minerals for the last year from Montana was considerable over $40,000,000. He had the output of each famous mine at his finger ends, and dazzled me with stories of marvelous dividends.

"Why, in Montana," he cried, "a business investment will bring all the way from fifteen to forty cents on the dollar, while in the East, what do you do? You worry along on a miserable six and one-half per cent., and imagine that you are becoming a millionaire when you get eight."

There was one thing I noticed here, and later about all the flourishing cities of the West. They are in love with electricity. Almost every town has a system of arc and incandescent lights, and many of them, Helena among the number, a line of electric street-cars.

Helena has the distinction of being the largest railroad center in Montana, and to this, perhaps, more than anything else, does she owe her wealth; for the mines of silver, of copper, and gold with which she is surrounded, would have been of comparatively little use to her without the roads which have made them accessible.

We spent one day visiting the Gates of the Rocky Mountains—where the Missouri cuts itself through a spur of the Belt Mountains between jagged and stupendous cliffs.

Wickes, Calvin, Rimini, and Marysville are the termini of three branches of the Northern Pacific which run from Helena. Each of these towns is the center of a mining district. The Drum Lummon mine, near Marysville, has the reputation of giving a yearly yield of $2,000,000 in gold and silver. In going from

MAMMOTH HOT SPRINGS HOTEL, YELLOWSTONE NATIONAL PARK.

Helena to Garrison one passes over the Rocky Mountain Divide, over the Mullan Pass; the pine and spruce decorate the rugged buttresses in an unavailing effort to soften their gauntness. I thought of my friend in corduroy as I learned of the game said to haunt these lonely forests and steep mountain-sides.

Taking the Montana Union Railway, a branch of the Northern Pacific, Mr. Bolter and I made our way to Butte. While I know that all that eastern men care to know about Butte can be answered by a series of figures, I am averse myself to speaking of this, the greatest mining city of the world, in just this manner; for I felt as if the air was filled with gold—there were fortunes and rumors of fortunes on every hand. Neither the house that a man lives in nor the clothes that he wears are any indication of his financial condition. Of what consequence are the possession of a few linen shirts more or less, when, before a year is over, one may be a millionaire several times told? If one must quote figures about Butte City, however, it is a comfort to know that these figures can be generous. The pay-roll of the men connected with the mines and smelters is at its minimum $500,000 a month, and it has been known to reach $870,000. It is said that no shaft was ever sunk in Butte which would not bring rich returns, if followed long enough. One mine in Butte—which has not the reputation of being any richer than several others, but from which I chanced to obtain figures—has paid $5,000,000 of dividends in eight years. The dividends of another mining company are $225,000 per month. Indeed, it seems impossible to even dig a ditch in this country without striking pay-dirt, and it is actually a fact that recently, in digging a sewer in the heart of the city, a lead of silver was struck which gives $280 per ton. I had always thought myself a fairly well-off man, but in this El Dorado, this community of millionaires, I had an impoverished feeling which for the first time made me wish to celebrate the honest virtues of low estate and poverty to sustain my self-love. The population of Butte is reckoned at about 25,000.

A short line branches from the Montana Union and runs to Anaconda, from which switch-backs and numerous tracks reach the smelter and concentrating works, which lie in two great groups on the side of the hills. The town lies in the sheltered valley among the brown mountains, its life being the great smelter and concentrating works. The output of copper here is greater than at any other point in the world. About 500 men are employed, directly or indirectly, by this enormous institution. The smelter is owned by a quartette of gentlemen, who, for the convenience of themselves and the large number of superintendents, chemists, etc., employed by them in the smelter, have erected a beautiful hotel, known as the Montana. It is exquisite in its appointments, and the service is unsurpassed. Erected at a cost of $250,000, it is, from the stand-point of the architect, the decorator, and the epicure, above criticism. The population is at present 6,000.

In neglecting to speak of the newspapers of the West, no disrespect is intended. The editors of these journals will take it for granted that it is only lack of space to do justice to the merits of their respective periodicals that induces this silence on the subject.

Returning to Garrison, which is the junction with the main line of the Northern Pacific Railroad, one passes through Deer Lodge, which, I am sure my corduroy friend would have been interested to know, derived its name from the vast herds of deer which used to wander through this valley. Rich grazing and farming lands lie round about, and the town serves as a general distributing point for the supplies for the mining district in the immediate vicinity. The scenery adjacent is not so grim as that about Butte and Helena. The landscape is relieved with trees, farms are luxuriant, and one receives the cheering assurance that there are numerous lakes and trout streams near by in the mountains. It was at Garrison that I received a letter from my sporting friend, a part of which I transcribe below:

"I have been following up the Yellowstone. I have been fishing in it! And the only thing that has detracted from my complete enjoyment is the fact that you were not with me—you who were designed by nature for the wielding of the rod. I have often heard it said that the first need of the fisherman was patience. But this does not hold good of the man that fishes in the Yellowstone. Here, nothing is needed but skill. I swear to you that in sixty minutes I landed eighteen fish, and I had my daintiest tackle, and gave a fair show to them.

"To feel the water rushing strong and cold against your legs, to feel your lungs swelling with that mountain air, to know the sudden and sweet sensation that is communicated from the line to your arm, and from your arm to your brain, when a bite comes, is one of the finest things in life, my boy—and you are missing it! I commiserate with you. You have missed your vocation. But I hope yet to see you with a rod in your hand.

"Fraternally yours,   PARKE."

The effect of this letter upon me was curious. At the outset of my acquaintance with Mr. Parke, I had lazily wondered how a man could take such a serious interest in matters as he did. Apparently, I had undergone a revulsion of feeling, for what I now wondered over was the fact that he could be so frivolous. It was evident that I was losing my indifference, and even against my will becoming interested in the West. But when my surroundings are taken into consideration, I am sure that even the most *blasé* will forgive me for my change of mind. For instance, I chanced to say to Mr. Bolter:

"Where does that Drummond & Phillipsburg Branch of the Northern Pacific run to?"

"Down to the Granite Mountain."

"What is the Granite Mountain?" I asked.

"It is a silver mine."

"Good for anything?" I asked.

"It has paid $3,000,000 in dividends," he said.

Then we both went on peeling pears, and I tried to conceal my sensations. I always did hate to show astonishment when I felt it.

Suddenly Bolter, helping himself to another pear, remarked :

"I wonder if you are a good collector of information?"

"Well," I said, "I am no reporter."

"Interested in horses?" said he.

"Of course," said I.

"I suppose you know, then, that the best race-track in the West is at Ana-conda?" I had to confess that I knew nothing of the sort.

"It is a magnificent track," he went on enthusiastically, "neither too hard nor too soft, and horses find the latitude so well adapted to them that it is nothing uncommon for a good horse to beat its record here. Another thing that you may or may not know is that Montana horses are beginning to make a reputation for themselves. I am glad to be able to tell you that there are a number of large horse ranches, where Kentucky trotting stallions and English and Norman draft stallions are used for breeding with native mares. The breeding of fine horses is becoming a remunerative industry in the Ter—State, I mean. The August meetings at Anaconda are becoming famous ; it is a sort of western Monmouth Park, in short. Last year there were sixty good horses entered, and it goes without saying that money was used freely enough;" and here he relapsed into a learned genealogical dissertation of a horsy nature, in which I was not able to follow him.

Still being in a speculative mood, we stopped at Missoula.

"I have heard of people," said my friend, "who followed summer round the earth. I am following the ever-engaging 'boom.'"

Now, a boom is associated to me with more or less discomfort, and when I saw the placid and hill-shielded town of Missoula, with its pleasant country homes, its broad streets and shaded yards, I could hardly believe it to be suffering from that peculiar form of commercial fever known to the western man by the uneuphonious name of "boom," and I found out later that in a sense I was right, for Missoula depends upon no fictitious values or unstable prosperity; for Mis-soula County lies in the midst of rich valleys, from which she will derive an ever-increasing strength. The Valley of the Bitter Root, over eighty miles long, the Jocko and Missoula Valleys, and many acres of fertile plains, are adjacent to Missoula, and at least seven rivers and creeks are in the immediate vicinity. Nothing richer or more beautiful than the Bitter Root Valley can be imagined, stretching out, as it does, between two lines of protecting mountains. Cherries, pears, quinces, apricots, grapes, strawberries, blackberries, and raspberries grow there to an unusual size, and have a flavor that is counted superior to that of the fruits of the Coast. So beautiful and so plenteous is this valley that were it not renowned for its productiveness, it certainly would be for its picturesqueness.

The Northern Pacific has under construction a branch line running from Missoula to connect at Mullan with its Cœur d'Alene system. This will give the Cœur d'Alene country direct outlet to the smelter at Helena, and incident-ally will, of course, be of much benefit to Missoula.

HOTEL BROADWATER, HELENA, ON N. P. R. R.

Two branch roads already leave Missoula, so that it is rapidly becoming commercially what it has ever been naturally, the center of the surrounding country. The richness of the district supplied by this ambitious town can be determined by the trade done in the village, and when it is stated that one merchandise company alone has a trade of over a million and a half a year, and finds market for everything from a bar of soap to the rarest imported laces, some idea of the financial condition of the country can be formed. Though the dwellings are of the sort commonly referred to as country houses, the business blocks, especially those in process of construction, are of metropolitan appearance, and represent an outlay that is the best guarantee of the town's prosperity. A garrison of United States troops is stationed at Fort Missoula. In the town is the Western Sanitarium of the Northern Pacific Beneficial Association, a commodious and well-equipped hospital for injured and sick employés. At present the town has a population of over 3,000.

After leaving Missoula, one sees the numerous buildings of the Flat Head Indian Reservation, where a Catholic mission exercises its kindly influence over two tribes of Indians and a large number of half-breeds. In the fruitful valley which it occupies irrigation is not needed, and the Reservation is noted for its picturesque cascades, lakes, and creeks. It is delightful to sit quietly, without the diversion of book or cigar, and, looking through the windows, watch the changing scenery of this region. Now one gets a bit of brown and mellow table-land, over which the buffalo used to roam; now one crosses a bridge high above some clear stream, or looks down the long vista of a valley beautified with mists and set in an amphitheatre of trees. Sometimes the track is blasted from solid rock, again it skirts the edge of a pellucid lake, or runs upon the edge of a precipitous hill. The place has the reputation for an abundance of game—which made me wonder at what point I was most likely to again meet with my friend in corduroy.

Once well over the Divide and on the western slope of the mountains, one becomes conscious of a milder atmosphere. The early morning air is tempered with something like balminess, and even at night, and in a high altitude, one is surprised to find that there is no need for shivering, although the month be September. It was my intention to visit the Cœur d'Alene Mountains—or rather the mines of that name—which lie in Idaho; but finding that they could be more conveniently reached from Spokane Falls than from any other point in the Territory of Idaho, I determined to delay my visit to that portion of country. My brief ride across the Territory is therefore principally associated in my mind with Lake Pend d'Oreille. For miles I had been looking at the tumultuous beauty of Clark's Fork, where it dashes its way through fluted chasms of rock, or tumbles over rocky beds in bright and exultant cascades. To leave this scene and come suddenly upon Lake Pend d'Oreille produces an entire revulsion of feeling. One has been all tumult, action, spontaneity; the other is the very embodiment of placidity. The forests that surround it seem interminable, and offer a thousand unexpected retreats and shelters in their secluded and beautiful bays. Mining camps and saw-mills furnish the evidences of industry. North of this, near the international line, lies one of the finest hunting territories on the American Continent.

We hastened on through the pleasant towns; through Hope, which has outgrown its appellation of a hunting resort; through Kootenai, from which roads run back into the Galena Mines on the Kootenai River; through Rathdrum, which is the center of a good cattle and timber country, to Hauser Junction, from which the Spokane Falls & Idaho Railroad diverges; this runs to Cœur d'Alene City. The 500 inhabitants of this town may be accounted especially fortunate in their selection of a town site, for it hangs over the lake of the same name, and has an exquisite picture spread before it continually. In every direction stretch the purple mountains of the Bitter Root and Cœur d'Alene ranges, and adjoining the town is Fort Sherman, upon Lake Cœur d'Alene, at an elevation that adds to its delights in times of peace as it would to its effectiveness in time of war. I doubt if there is a military post in the country so beautifully situated. Steamboats run from Cœur d'Alene City up the lake and river of the same name to Mission, where I learned that they connect with trains running to Wardner, Wallace, and Mullan, which are among the richest mining towns of the district. A connecting line is being constructed by the Northern Pacific, which will do away with the need for steamboat transportation, except in the event of opening up the Cœur d'Alene Reservation, a portion of which Congress has arranged to purchase. Should this occur, a rich agricultural and mining country, on both sides of the lake and river, will be thrown open to settlers.

Had I followed my inclination, I should have left the main road at Hauser Junction, and taken the alluring ride up the lake and river which was so vividly described to me by a fellow passenger. I was in great danger here of losing my speculative friend, who was fascinated by the tales of wealth in these mountains, and I should have been glad to have visited the old mission church, which, they told me, presents a chaste façade of the Italian style, built under the direction of the venerable Father Ravalli, although his Indian workmen had nothing but axes and whip-saws with which to construct it.

At Wardner, Burke, and Mullan there has been a wonderful development of silver that has quite overshadowed the original camp that made the Cœur d'Alene country famous. That original camp was at Murray, and the mining, as everyone knows, was placer gold mining. I remember, in this connection, hearing that, twelve or fourteen years ago, Butte was known only as a placer camp, even as the Cœur d'Alene country was known as a placer region through the original discoveries on Pritchard's Creek. It is the opinion of experienced miners—so my speculative friend declared with excited gestures—that the camps at Wardner, Burke, and Mullan will rival if not excel anything of the kind in the world. The stores of ore are so numerous as to be practically inexhaustible; and the probable completion next year of the Northern Pacific's line between Mullan and Missoula, already referred to, will give new interest to the development of this remarkable region.

The mining camps of the Cœur d'Alene district contain about 20,000 people. A strange place and a strange people! I should say that they were all intoxicated with success. There is gold in the very air. One feels rich whether he has a cent in his pocket or not. It is as impossible to be slow or dull in a place like this, as it is to be dry when one is up to one's neck in water.

Full of new and pleasant enthusiasm, I entered Spokane Falls. It was still in the chaos that followed the great fire. The streets were blockaded with building materials. The directory was valueless. One-half of the business portion of the town was still in tents, and one of the leading churches had been pressed into the government service and was used as a post-office. I had difficulty in finding a place in which to lay my head, for all the hotels having been burned, the boarding-houses were crowded with the army of workmen, business-men, and sight-seers who had been drawn to the place.

I do not feel that I have a very clear idea of what Spokane Falls was before the catastrophe, or what it may be in the future; I only know that I came away fascinated with the fortitude, the optimism, and the energy which could so quickly build up a new city on the spot of a deserted one, and do it, too, in a manner that seemed to imply that the builders were gratified by having some obstacle to overcome, and that they measured success only by the difficulties encountered. Like Monte Cristo, the people of Spokane Falls appeared to think that "the world was theirs." With magnificent anticipations, they had laid out lots far over the swelling spruce-clad hills that stretched beyond the town. A cable-car line runs on a substantial double bridge across a picturesque ravine, and into this same uninhabited and most picturesque and desirable country.

But to return to the city itself; its strength lies in the Falls. There built a village long before the railroad came into the country. They have been estimated at 216,000 horse-power. The town rises gradually from the bank of the Spokane River until it reaches a line of bluffs, which are nearly a mile from the shore; then northward stretches a level plain, and here the best part of the State stands. But around the Falls centers the interest of the commercial man and the tourist alike. The waters have three different paths for themselves, and they come pouring over the ledges with a force mighty enough to work all the looms, the spindles, the grinders, and the engines that are needed for the city. Saw-mills and flour-mills, sash and door factories, fence works, carriage works, an oatmeal mill, a pottery, and the cable-car power-house already cluster around them.

Spokane Falls is by far the most important railroad center in Eastern Washington. The Spokane Falls & Idaho reaches into the Cœur d'Alene country; the Spokane & Palouse runs into the famous Palouse wheat region, its ultimate destination being Lewiston; and the Spokane Falls & Northern taps the Colville Valley, which also has a wide reputation for a heavy yield of

CŒUR D'ALENE LAKE AND STEAMER "CŒUR D'ALENE."

wheat and small grains. But what can one write of a city in the condition of
Spokane Falls? Everything is in a state of transition. The town has many
beautiful residences, and they are daily being added to. Work has been begun
on a $300,000 opera-house, and several excellent hotels are in process of con-
struction. The water-works system of the city is capable of supplying 12,000,000
gallons daily; and the machinery of these extensive works is also run by the
water-power.

It was at Spokane Falls that I received a shock. I was standing near the
Falls, looking at the rapidly rising walls of the new hotel—a hotel which is to be
erected at a cost of $250,000—when suddenly I felt a hand on my shoulder.
A man stood beside me in blue-jean overalls and a knitted jersey.

" Not out of a job, are you, pard?" he said.

" Why no," I said, " I am not."

" Thought you was," says he, " seein' you stand 'round."

Evidently I was the only idle man in Spokane. But up to this time I had
supposed my faultless costume would protect me from such suspicion. Imagine
my surprise, then, when I paused in my wild career for information to take an
inventory, so to speak, of myself. My boots were covered with mud, my silk
hat had given place to an ounce hat, which was decorated with the dust of
several States and Territories. I had caught the admiration for the flannel shirt
which seems to possess men of all stations in the West, and my elaborately
knotted tie had given way to a convenient loop of silk. The coat which I
used to wear ceremoniously buttoned now flapped in the wind, and there was
something in the atmosphere which made me feel that I no longer had time to
draw on and button any of the numerous pairs of gloves which I had selected,
before my departure, with so much care.

" How many men are there of you engaged in putting this city together
again?" I asked my new acquaintance.

" There are 3,500 of us," he said, " if there is a man; we call ourselves the
' Boys in Blue,'" he said, slapping one blue-jean leg, " and before the year is
over we'll have put $4,000,000 worth of brick and mortar together."

I saw next to nothing of my speculative friend, Mr. Bolter, during my
so'ourn at Spokane Falls. He was engaged in a search for corner lots, compared to which Sir Galahad's search for the Holy Grail was as nothing in its
devotion.

" What do you find on the hills?" Mr. Bolter cried to me, as we ate our
early breakfast together. " Yellow pine, cedar, tamarack, and white pine! Magnificent woods, every one of them, sir. And what do you get in rivers?—
the finest water-power in the world. Look at the population of 22,000—in 1883
there were only 800 people here. At that ratio, in the next three years this will
be a city of 75,000. Then think of the mining districts! There is Cœur
d'Alene, the Colville, the Kootenai, and the Okanogan, all directly tributary to
the town. Not old mining districts worked out, mind you, but fresh fields,

which only need capital and energy to develop them ; and it is the very home of enterprise, sir. At this minute, there are three new churches going up, not one of which will cost less than $30,000. The Northern Pacific are putting up a fine passenger depot. Everything is humming here, sir. There is good blood here, sir—good newspapers, good water—good everything. I have just clipped a statement from that very excellent paper, the *Spokane Falls Review*, to the effect that the Northern Pacific is by 425 miles the shortest line from Chicago and the East to Spokane. This has been recently added to by the Little Falls Cut-off, which is newly completed. Don't you dare to leave this town without appreciating it." I am sure I did not; no one could.

But instead of taking the main trunk of that road, for which Mr. Bolter had so sincere an admiration, I determined to journey down into the famous Palouse country. I have no pleasanter associations with any part of my journey than with those long and careless days that I spent driving from point to point over these hills. The Palouse Valley contains a hundred valleys, at this season of the year golden with ripe grain. I had laughed when they told me that wheat in the Palouse Valley averaged from thirty to forty bushels an acre; but one ceases to disbelieve, in looking at these tremendous fields of grain, in which a man might without difficulty lose his way. The towns in the Palouse Valley center around the elevators where the wheat is kept; the railroads are built to carry away the wheat; the roads are lined with the interminable fields of plenty. I was surprised at the small number of granaries that I saw, and learned that it was the custom to sell the grain before winter, packing it from the nearest station in bags. I shall always remember my journey through this land of plenty. One can tire of awing mountain views, and find in the placid undulations of wholesome plains a comfort and a rest. I might have returned to Cheney, the prosperous junction, which has a record of wheat shipments amounting to $100,000 a year, but I chose to economize time and space by taking a cross-country line, which returned me to the Northern Pacific at Connell.

How could I marvel now at the recuperative power and the apparent wealth of Spokane Falls? What the Palouse country was, I had seen. What the Big Bend country, tributary to it from the other direction, was, I had heard. This country, embraced by the Columbia, sends down wheat scarcely inferior to the Palouse region. Grasses, vegetables, and small fruits grow there to a degree, but wheat, as in the Palouse country, is the chief product. Stock-raising, however, which is enterprisingly carried on in the Big Bend country, is not known in the Palouse district. Beef-cattle sell, in this district, for from $30 to $40 per head; a team of horses for $200; and the capricious but invaluable cayuse, for from $5 to $30; and this leads me to say, parenthetically, that the cayuse is the least appreciated of animals. It is true that it is necessary to become in sympathy with the cayuse, but when once he has been persuaded that he is carrying a perfectly respectable member of society, and one interested in the future of the country, there is no limit to the number of miles that he will patiently and safely carry him.

As I journeyed westward, I met with a phenomena. If I innocently picked up a picture floating about on a platform or hanging from a peg, I was advised in scarlet letters to "keep my eye on Pasco." Every traveling-man on the road supplemented his "good morning" with an inquiry as to whether or not I was keeping my eye on Pasco. Therefore, as we approached Pasco, I delayed my meal, notwithstanding the vigorous appetite, for the purpose of doing as directed. I found Pasco the point of divergence for the Cascade Division of the Northern Pacific Railroad; in other words, here the two lines, coming from Portland and Tacoma, meet. A great man had prophesied that this would be the point of a future city, and here the young city was, not out of swaddling-clothes yet, but a most precocious and healthy infant, with a well-developed pair of lungs, and its outreaching hand on the first rung of the ladder of fame.

Shortly after this we passed, in the deepening dusk, the great bridge that spans Snake River, the construction of which would have been gratifying to the appreciative eye of my friend Bolter, had he been with me. Hunt's Junction—to follow up the road, as Bolter would have me—is the connecting point with the Northern Pacific of two lines of the Oregon & Washington Railroad, both of which traverse the wheat country, one extending to Walla Walla, Waitsburg, and Dayton, Washington, and the other to Pendleton, Oregon, all points of commercial importance, Walla Walla being a city of 5,000 or 6,000 people, and of some historic renown. Occasionally tourists go to Portland via Wallula Junction and the Columbia River line, but as the views along the Columbia can best be seen from the river—as I myself found out later—the majority of the sightseers go direct to Portland by way of the Cascade Division of the Northern Pacific, making the journey along the Columbia River from Portland by boat as far as the Dalles, returning by rail to Portland. This is a journey that occupies but a day. Hunt's Junction is, I believe, important, not only because of its facilities for accommodating travelers who wish to reach the Columbia River towns, but also because the Hunt lines tap the very heart of Eastern Washington, and deliver to the Northern Pacific Road, at the junction, a very large portion of the wheat production of the district referred to. This wheat is carried by the Northern Pacific over its Cascade Division to Tacoma. I must say, parenthetically, that I am very proud of the way I now was able to collect facts, and I felt that Bolter would have been proud of me if he had known about it. By the way, it was here that a depressed farmer informed me that crops in Walla Walla district had been poor—the poorest in the history of the country, the average in wheat being only twenty bushels an acre. In short, Walla Walla would ship only 2,500,000 bushels of wheat, and this, he estimated, would take 4,534 freight cars, of fifteen tons capacity each, to move the wheat, and, if each of the two roads move fifty cars each day, two months of steady work will be necessary to haul the grain. I may remark, incidentally, here, that later I

"THE POORMAN"—CŒUR D'ALENE MINING DISTRICT, BURKE, IDAHO.

chanced to come across an estimate of the wheat crop of Washington for the year 1889. Six hundred thousand acres were planted, producing 10,000,000 bushels, the worth of which is $6,500,000.

I was in a good humor as I approached Yakima, for Yakima, so I had heard, was a very determined and pugilistic young city. When she wanted a thing, she wanted it bad enough to fight for it, and she even had the reputation of getting what she wanted. At present, she chanced to be wanting the legislative seat of the young State. She was going to be capital or nothing.

It was as the train pulled into Yakima that I met with a young man who has since become one of my warmest friends. Permit me to refer to him as the Young Poet. I suspected his avocation at once, for, though the poets of the present day do not wear Byronic collars, or indulge in hyacinthine locks, the trade-marks are the same as they were in the early part of the century. His first remark to me confirmed my suspicions.

"This," said he, "is where the South and the North are married." I was not in a mood to be sympathetic, and I regarded this enthusiastic youth with a cold stare.

"Really," I said, "what may that mean?"

"It means," said he, "that the products of the North and of the South grow equally well in the Valley of the Yakima."

"Oh," I said, "I suppose you mean to say they have sorghum and yams up here?"

"Precisely," said he; "the tobacco-flower blooms here beside the bearded grain—I have written a few lines upon the subject."

"Thank you," I said, "I should be delighted to hear them, but unfortunately I get off here."

"Ah," cried he, joyfully, "so do I. Come with me, and we will go to the Hotel Yakima together, and as we go I will read you my 'Apostrophe' to the twelve valleys which pay tribute to the Yakima."

By keeping up a supply of well-directed conversation, I managed to avert this evil, as we drove up the broad and tidy street of Yakima to the hospitable inn which bears the name of the town. But notwithstanding my utmost efforts to avoid the Young Poet, I found myself sitting opposite him at dinner, and, after completing my inspection of the menu, was obliged to peruse the following—a tribute to the young man's recently adopted town, and the principal river which flows through it:

Brown are the hills by the Yakima,
Brown through the blue of the swathing mist,
And the sturdy points of the topmost peaks
By the clouds of the brooding sky are kist.

Clear is the flow of the Yakima,
And cold as the snows that feed its source,
And wherever it flows through the wholesome plains,
Unstintingly lends from its splendid force.

It waters the waste, does the Yakima,
  And the desert bursts in bloom like the rose;
It sings as it turns the miller's wheel,
  And it washes the gold from the dross as it flows.

" I am the sorrowless Yakima,"
  So sings the stream, while the ages run;
" I am the servant of plenty and peace,
  Born of the love of the snow and the sun."

Faithful and true is the Yakima,
  And broad is the valley it flows to bless,
And the mountains drink in their cups of snow,
  An eternal toast to its deathlessness.

This might have widened the breach between us, but I knew that I was not free from faults myself, and promised to be friends with him if he would not talk shop—poetry being, of course, the " shop " of poets.

" What I want to know about," I told him, " is the resources of the country. The Young Poet sniffed the air disdainfully.

" I dare say the hotel clerk can instruct you," he said. But I went out and gathered information from other sources. I found that every preparation had been made there for a desirable city. On each side of the wide streets were planted rows of trees, and the mountain streams have been coaxed to run through ditches by the roadway. The population is about 2,500. It has tasteful churches, a remarkably imposing school building, sixty-five business houses, and two banks, each of which claim a daily deposit of $6,500.

As to the natural resources of the country, I learned that the clay round about was so well adapted for brick-making that Yakima sported two large brick-yards; excellent anthracite coal had been discovered thirty-five miles west; in the northeast, only twenty-five miles distant, were gold and silver mines, and a stamp mill; and good horse ranches are in the vicinity. Although Yakima is surrounded with mountains, it is accessible by five convenient passes, of which the people of Yakima hope more than one railroad company will yet avail themselves. But the pride of Yakima is its irrigated farms. I drove out to the Moxee farm, about three miles from the village, where I saw an illustration of what can be done with these sage-brush lands, which look so repulsive to the eye of an eastern man. Here there are 2,000 acres under cultivation. Forty-five acres are laid out in hops, which produce 16,000 pounds to an acre. Two crops of wheat are raised a year, the spring wheat averaging thirty-five bushels to an acre, and one field yielding fifty. Five crops of alfalfa and five of clover are raised. Sorghum and peanuts, squashes, melons, and corn, grow in friendly juxtaposition. The peaches of this district have as delicious a flavor as I ever tasted. But what surprised me most was the twenty-five acres of tobacco, and the great steaming-house where the leaves were prepared for use. A number of cigar-makers are employed, and before this beloved weed leaves the Moxee Valley it is made into three brands of cigars, which I do protest are as good as any domestic cigars that it has ever been my privilege to smoke. From 3,000 to 4,000 head of stock are raised on the Moxee farm, and not far from there I

visited the excellent dairy of Mr. Henry B. Scudder, who manufactures butter
and cheese enough to satisfy the local market. Before long it is probable that
systematic irrigation will be undertaken, thus putting in cultivation 500,000
acres of land immediately around Yakima. The young orchards will also be
greatly benefited by this, and in the near future the Yakima Basin may become
one of the best fruit countries in the West. I was advised by the Young Poet
to visit the Titan Basin, fifty miles southeast of Yakima, where, according to
his description, exquisite falls break from glacial rivers into a green valley of
wonderful loveliness. They told me, too, of the soda springs, where the people of
Yakima resort in summer to breathe the air of the Pacific as it sweeps across the
mountains; but I determined to hasten on, after having made elaborate notes in
my memorandum-book concerning watermelons which weighed fifty-four pounds
apiece, squashes which weighed eighty-six, sorghum which grew ten feet high,
corn which went it one foot better, hop vines which presented solid clusters
of fruit forty feet long, and oats which grew six feet high and rustled a bearded
head two feet in length.

A short journey of two hours' duration brings one to Ellensburg, a rival town,
which is also ambitious to be the capital of the new State, in the stead of
Olympia. This is a matter that will take two years, and several castings of
ballots, to decide upon. Ellensburg has the advantage of Yakima in point of
population; it claims 4,000, which is, perhaps, a modest estimate. The business portion of the town having been destroyed by fire, nearly a million and a
half of property has been lost during the past year.

But the wonderful buoyancy of the West is seen in this town, as in Spokane
and Seattle. Ellensburg is rich in manufacturing interests for a town of its size,
having one foundry, which supplies castings for many of the cities of Eastern
Washington, three flouring-mills, three planing-mills, a sash and door factory,
a galvanized-iron establishment, and the Falls of the Yakima River to furnish
power. Public schools, hotels, and large office buildings are being erected
with that rapidity which no longer surprises me; but it seems to be as natural
to western enterprise as caution is to the business ventures of the city.

There are two exceedingly prosperous banks here, which is not surprising,
the town lying, as it does, in the midst of agricultural and mining country.
Ellensburg hopes to be the junction point with the main line of the Central
Washington Branch of the Northern Pacific, now building from Cheney through
the Big Bend country toward the Columbia River. It is also probable that a
branch will be thrown northward from this Central Washington Road toward
Lakes Chelan and Okanogan. The natural advantages of this town can be
judged by the fact that eight miles northeast lie rich bituminous coal mines,
which furnish the same quality of coal as the famous Roslyn mines. Iron ore
has been discovered in the northern part of the county, and on the Swauk
River are placer mines, which require only water to make them pay well. There
are 1,000 square miles of rich agricultural country, on which wheat averages

SPOKANE RIVER AND FALLS

thirty-five bushels to the acre, and not infrequently reaches extraordinary figures of from fifty to fifty-five bushels. Barley and oats yield from fifty-five to sixty-eight bushels per acre. Vegetables of all sorts grow abundantly, and potatoes have the reputation of being unrivaled. (Again I made annotations in my note-book concerning cabbages which weighed forty-six pounds, onions which measured twenty-one inches, and smelled to Heaven, and apples which no one but a Titan might undertake to bite.)

The frost is over early in May, and begins about the first of October, no snow falling until Christmas; but the impatient farmers feel that they are justified in plowing their fields early in February. The uplands are excellent for grazing; and from here the Sound derives nearly its entire supply of cattle. At one shipment, just before my visit, Ellensburg had forwarded 3,500 sheep to Tacoma and the surrounding towns. It is unnecessary to say that Ellensburg, Yakima, and all other towns mentioned and to be mentioned, are well supplied with newspapers, of various political faiths, and all devoted to the development of the Great West. We passed Cleahum and Roslyn, two towns which subsist upon the famous coal mines bearing the name of the latter town, and reached the great tunnel of Stampede Pass. Nine thousand eight hundred and fifty feet is this tunnel, with a grade of thirty-nine feet to the mile.

Joaquin Miller passed through here the other day, though in the opposite direction, and wrote something about it, which I chanced to pick up. Here it is, in the poet's peculiar phraseology:

"About 500 miles of sun and snow, of sand and sage-brush, of burning desert and of bristling peaks, a variety of clime and of scene such as would not be encountered in the journey from London to Jerusalem, and the trouble is not what to say, as you look back over this long, swift dash from tide-water to the interior of this new State of Washington, but what not to say.

"The first few hours out from Tacoma you are in a narrow path between impenetrable walls of moss-hung and overhanging trees. A dimple now and then to right or left, a little of a house and barn, a hop-field, a few fat cows belly-deep in grass and flowers, great thickets of grapes, wild and tame, a flashing trout-stream away down under the trellis or wooden bridge, and that is all you see or know of the thousands upon thousands of square miles that make up the great wood-world, Washington.

"After a while we pull up, a rattle and a clank, the shout and puff and groan of our weary engine, and then two monstrous big creatures, two huge black engines, such as were never seen in the States, I reckon, come steaming out from the round-house; and we know there is heavy work on hand—we are about to climb the Oregon Sierras, and pierce their summits by the route of the great tunnel of the Northern Pacific Railroad, only recently completed. We pass one, two, five, ten, twenty great lumber mills; strings of oxen half a mile long; little armies of men with ax and saw and ox-whip. I tell you it is a busy place, this Washington wood-world!

"Get land, get land, get land here—lumber land: for California, Nevada, the plains, all the civilized world, wants lumber to build with."

I subscribe a very excellent editorial which I found in the pages of the

North-Western Magazine, and which describes, as well as anything I have seen, the condition of Seattle, to which I was now hastening, leaving the main road at Meeker:

"The great fire of June 6th in Seattle was as terrible a calamity in proportion to the size of that city as was the historic Chicago fire; indeed, it was even more serious, for in Chicago a portion of the business district was saved, while in Seattle everything was destroyed except the residence quarters. The business streets were completely wiped out by the flames. Every hotel, every bank, every newspaper office, and every store was consumed. The wharves, depots, electric railway, cable line, warehouses, saw-mills, and factories, all shared in the ruin. In short, the entire business plant of a city of 25,000 inhabitants, constructed by twenty years of enterprise, and representing a value of perhaps $20,000,000, was devoured in a few hours by the flames.

"The citizens of Seattle are wonderfully cheerful in the face of this tremendous misfortune. In time their city will be the gainer by the fire, as Chicago was, for they will permit no buildings to be erected in the business district that are not reasonably safe. In their new plans for building they will doubtless banish all saw-mills and lumber-yards from the center of the city; will provide terminal grounds for railroads, the want of which has heretofore been seriously felt; and will secure a better wharf system than the old one, which had gradually expanded with the needs of a growing commerce. There is now a good opportunity for intelligently reshaping the commercial heart of the city, so as to give it facilities adequate for future demands. The losses fall heavily upon individuals, but the city itself is too vital not to recover from the blow. In two years there will be very few signs remaining in Seattle to tell of the great conflagration."

Seattle slopes on a succession of terraces down to the exquisite harbor formed by the inreaching arm of Puget's Sound, surrounding the city on three sides. A little way back from the city, north, south, and east, stretch great valleys. King County, of which Seattle is the county-seat, is said to contain as much mineral wealth in iron and coal as the better part of Pennsylvania. Hops in King County yield 2,000 pounds to the acre, and have been known to reach 4,000 pounds.

I did not know that I had an acquaintance among the 30,000 inhabitants of this beautiful city, but what was my surprise and delight to find in one of the most stirring young commercial gladiators of the place a distant kinsman of mine; but for his name, I certainly never should have recognized in this business-like and self-sufficient young gentleman the pale and scrawny youth who left New York five years before. This handsome young man was so pressed for time, that, though he was willing to show me everything in the city and be courteous to the utmost limit of his power, he would talk in nothing but broken sentences.

"Come up to club," said he; "talk over things."

We lunched there together in apartments which even an old New York club

man like myself could find nothing to criticise; and as for the club-men themselves, I thought I never had struck such candid, hospitable, energetic, and sen-
sible a lot of fellows. They were college-bred and traveled, most of them; but
they were not, as one of them put it, "traveling upon their shapes." In fact, I
soon found out that men in Washington are taken for what they are, and not for
what their fathers might have been.

"Great place, Seattle," said my kinsman in jerks, as he cut his salad.
"Never mean to leave it. Know what I was when I came out here? Office boy.
Swept out bank. All right now, though. President of bank and I went into
partnership. Want to know real-estate transfers of Seattle, from January 1st,
1889, to September 1st? $10,443,661.50. All right now, you know. Don't
sweep out office any more."

After luncheon we went out to drive. We drove out to Lake Washington,
as dainty a bit of liquid turquoise as was ever set in a band of hills. By Lake
Union stands Queen Anne town, one of the fashionable suburbs, and up hill
and down are the residences, the school-houses, the churches, of this ambitious
town. To accommodate the transportation of this ambitious place, the Northern Pacific Road has recently constructed a freight depot 750 feet in length.

"Can't crush us with a $20,000,000 fire," said my kinsman. "Look at our
wharves, will you. Ever see such coal bunkers? We've four newspapers, and
they're mighty good ones; we've three lines of electric cars and four cable
lines. That foundation right there," he said, pointing to a structure that stood
on a pleasant spot overlooking Elliot Bay, "is the Hotel Denny, going to cost
$50,000."

The day was intensely clear, the sky almost unbelievably blue; out on the
bay glimmered the white sails, and not far distant, across the ferry, rose the
green heights of West Seattle. The shining peaks of Mounts Tacoma, Baker,
Adams, and St. Helens pierced the bright sky. I added to all this visible
beauty the knowledge that I had of the country adjacent, of the mountain of
iron, of the Snoqualmie Valley, which produces excellent hops, of the forests so
dense that the country within a radius of forty miles of Seattle sends out one-
half as much lumber annually as the States of Wisconsin and Michigan com-
bined, and I concluded that this was a city any man might be proud to live in.

On my way to Seattle I had passed through the Puyallup Valley in the
night, and therefore I had little opportunity of seeing this famous region. I
therefore lingered about Puyallup for several days. The hops were ripening,
though not yet ready for harvest. Mile upon mile stretched the picturesque
fields of hops, their graceful streamers reaching from pole to pole till one could
imagine he saw a company of green-clad spirits of the fields engaged in some
charming dance. It is sixteen years since the valley of the Puyallup was planted
with hops, and during this entire time there has never been a failure of crops.
In the autumn the Indians from the adjacent Reservation and from the coast
come here by the thousand to gather the harvest. Indeed, afterward, far north-

FARM AND HOP YARD, NORTH YAKIMA, WASH.

ward on my Alaskan journey, I saw fleets of long canoes laden with Alaskan Indians bound southward for Puyallup.

The ride that brought me to Tacoma was a short one.

It was early morning, and I went at once to that excellent hostelry, the "Tacoma." After breakfast, I sat out on the piazza overlooking the stretch of tide lands, and read two articles which had been given to me by my Seattle kinsman, in a fit of generous admiration for this rival town. The first was a description of the town by Joaquin Miller; the second, a bit of clever essay writing by that unfortunate young poet and novelist, Theodore Winthrop, who was one of the first victims of the Rebellion. Here is the letter from the "Poet of the Sierras:"

"This is a red town—more red than Washington City, with her endless avenues of red brick and her continuous trees, which serve to emphasize the red with the contrasting green. The city is built of red brick, with limestone rock in the rough for a first story as a rule. But besides the red brick, the roofs of the houses are painted red; and as the city is on a hill, with the blue waters of the inland sea before her, and a crescent of dense green forest crowding close around and closing in to right and left, why, you see, Tacoma is a tower and a battlement of red, brilliant by contrast with sky and sea and somber wilderness.

"I told you in my last I should walk over this red city set on a hill, and count down in cold figures exactly the number of brick houses I should find in the course of construction. I counted something more than 200, when I was overtaken by the mayor of the city. I told him what I was about, and asked for figures and facts. As new ground is being broken daily, and in different parts of the place, I could not get quite what I desired without going over the entire town—a too considerable task with the streets in their present crowded and incomplete condition. But the official count of houses built the past year is a little over 1,000. This is enough to show you that Tacoma is a fact, an impetuous and a formidable fact!

"This youngest and strongest of all the young cities of the Union is ninety-eight miles by water road from the ocean, and about forty miles from the Pacific as the crow flies.

"The cars creep along under her on the edge of the water, just as they do at Vicksburg. In fact, Tacoma looks not unlike Vicksburg before the war, if we leave out the color and activity. Her location is very much like that of Vicksburg, and the inland sea is not much wider than is the Mississippi at that point. But we are at the head of the sea here, or the 'Sound,' as it is called; and you do not see the passing steamers and rafts and flatboats, as when you look down from the heights of Vicksburg on the Father of Waters. Still there are plenty of ships, some of them from far away, from the under-world, waiting for wheat, hops, and lumber. A continuous stream of coal is pouring out from this port now. The increase of exports of this place during this year over the year preceding already amounts to $3,000,000.

"I find eight banks here; and the school-house, college, and church, as is usually the case where the American pioneer plants the banner of progress, are even more conspicuous than the money centers. Down out of the semi-environment of dense forests there come continually from five different directions the long and laden strings of cars. And I never saw cars so crowded.

" 'You must telegraph ahead for rooms.'

" 'What! and twenty-two hotels in Tacoma?'

" I did not telegraph. I have slept under the trees too often to resort to the foppish and affected custom of taking too much care of self, as do many worthless Americans. And so, after tramping about the town for a long time, grip-bag in hand, I was about to set out for the nearest woods, where I saw a forest fire in full glory, when a stranger kindly volunteered to give me shelter.

" But among the many edifices in the course of construction there are hotels enough, let it be hoped, to care for all who come in the near future. And while on this subject, let me say that the food is abundant here; not only is it abundant, but it is well cooked and well served. And for fear that I have given the broad impression that this is a sort of mining camp, so far as comfort is concerned, I must write it down that now, as the laden steamer has sailed away for Alaska and left room for me, I have secured quarters in a hotel so elegant that I am filled with astonishment at its perfection. You would mistake this airy red hostelry for a palace of the middle ages. Now, this is saying very much for a city so new that it continually smells of paint whichever way you pass as you walk the streets; but I know what I am about. The edifice is a copy from Ancona, I should say. At least, I am certain I have seen its airy red counterpart—its high, light gables, its tile imitations, its countless curves and turns of roof and wall and corner—by the banks of the Adriatic Sea, or somewhere along there, in and about Ancona or Ravenna.

" These hotels are not crowded thus by those who are building the city. The strangers on the balconies that look out on the inland sea from this island of red are, as a rule, merely the better class of seaside loungers. I should say that the greater portion of those who fill the first-class houses here at this season of the year are the wealthier and healthier of the Newport and Long Branch people, who, with a bit of an eye to business in the way of land speculation, are merely taking a longer 'run' down to the seaside. Certain it is that I see the same quiet manners here, the same absence of care and business concern that marks the well-bred American at our famous sea resorts on the other side of the Republic. And I have met two men here whom I saw at Newport not many years ago."

Less spectacular, but equally graphic, are the words in which Lieutenant Winthrop, more than a score of years ago, described the stately mountain which, even as I read his words, rose before me, flushing and shimmering under the morning sun, to bear witness to the truth of his eloquence.

He is speaking of Mount Tacoma, and says:

" The range continues dark and rough, and sometimes unmeaning to the eye, until it is relieved by Tacoma—*vulgo* Regnier. * * * Kingly and alone stood this majesty, without any visible comrade or consort, though far to the north and south its brethren and sisters dominated their realms, each in isolated sovereignty, rising above the pine-darkened sierra of the Cascade Mountains; above the stern chasm where the Columbia—Achilles of rivers—sweeps, short-lived and jubilant, to the sea; above the lovely vales of the Willamette and Umpqua. Of all the peaks from California to Fraser River, this one before me was royalest. Mount Regnier, Christians have dubbed it, in stupid nomenclature, perpetuating the name of somebody or nobody. More melodiously, the Siwashes call it Tacoma. * * * * * *

" No foot of man had ever trampled those pure snows. It was a virginal mountain, distant from the possibility of human approach and human inquisitiveness as a marble goddess is from human loves. Yet there was nothing unsympathetic in its isolation, or despotic in its distant majesty. But this serene loftiness was no home for any deity of those that men create. Only the thought of eternal peace arose from this heaven-upbearing monument, like incense, and, overflowing, filled the world with deep and holy calm. Wherever the mountain turned its cheek toward the sun, many fair and smiling dimples appeared, and along soft curves of snow lines of shadow drew tracery fair as the blue veins on a child's temple. Without the infinite sweetness and charm of this kindly changefulness of form and color, there might have been oppressive awe in the presence of this transcendent glory against the solemn blue of noon. Grace played over the surface of majesty, as a drift of rose leaves wavers in the air before the grandeur of a storm. Loveliness was sprinkled, like a boon of blossoms, upon sublimity.

"Studying the light and the majesty of Tacoma, there passed from it, and entered into my being—to dwell there evermore, by the side of many such—a thought and an image of solemn beauty, which I could thenceforth evoke whenever in the world I must have peace, or die. For such emotion, years of pilgrimage were worthily spent."

With these words still in my brain, I went out to walk about the "red city." Through the busy streets I went, wondering if indeed I were in that young town whose name a short time before had been unknown to me; for I should have had no difficulty in fancying myself on the streets of some old and long-prosperous city, except for the restless force that seemed to animate everyone. On one corner stood a great "red" building, with a stately tower—the new opera-house; on another, a granite business block—indeed, they were on every side—half-finished edifices, rising in comely substantiality among those which, already completed, give to the streets of Tacoma their metropolitan appearance. Someone told me that $100,000 was being expended on that beautiful opera-house building. I went past the wharves, on up toward the hill. No one could help stopping there for a while, if only to look over that stretch of limpid water. But, besides the bay, there were the ships from a dozen lands, flying their flags in the bright morning air. Afterward, when I learned that the wheat shipments of Tacoma for the year 1889 were little short of 6,000,000 bushels, I was not astonished—for is not Tacoma the greatest port for the shipment of wheat in the world? Then the great coal bunkers still growing with the passing of the season—in which $57,000 have been spent—spoke of another source of wealth. The flag of Japan waved out there in the harbor by the side of a vessel from Baltimore, which had made its way round the dreaded Horn. Here were the evidences of wealth and prosperity before my eyes! I walked on up the hill, refusing to take the steam motors that rushed by me, and thinking of all that these western men had to be proud of. Here, on the hill, stood the fairest homes that I had ever seen. It was not that they represented an outlay of more money, although many of them were costly, but they stood, so daintily fashioned in the latest caprice of fashionable architecture, in scenes so calculated to set off their picturesqueness,

PEACH ORCHARD, NORTH YAKIMA, WASH

that the effect was something, taken as a whole, that I had never seen excelled. The fir-clad hills stretched far beyond. The bay lay shimmering in perennial blueness below. The vine-draped bluffs dropped down to them, and to the ships at anchor. And in among gardens and lawns stood the homes of Tacoma, well kept, verandahed, hospitable, among churches and schools and pleasant drives. It was then that I recollected the letter given me by the old judge, back in St. Paul, to his son. The recollection was prompted, I suppose, by a desire to enter one of those gracious dwellings. I determined to present it at once.

I found the young attorney without difficulty. He was a blonde gentleman, not yet past twenty-five winters, clad in the lightest and neatest of garments. Indeed, his whole appearance betokened amiability. The smile with which he greeted me, the very color of his garments, the elegance of his red gold moustache, all added to the impression. We talked at length of Tacoma and its prospects.

"Tacoma," said he, flipping a bit of dust from his polished boot, "has every reason for succeeding, and none for doing otherwise. This year the Northern Pacific will expend $880,000 in improvements here, which is only a small part of the money they stand pledged to expend for the city; $30,000 per month are now being expended in the way of grading streets and laying sidewalks; $600,000 will be the sum total paid by the Tacoma Light & Water Company on its system. The new smelting works are costing $200,000, and have a capacity of 150 tons of ore per day. The saw-mills—which you must visit with me—have an average output of 980,000 feet a day, the value of which is $3,500,000 per year. And we sell this in Australia, the Sandwich Islands, China, Japan, California, and the Mississippi Valley. But why bore you with these details? Tacoma speaks for herself; she needs no oration from me. Stay here a week, and you will never want to leave."

Just at this moment a young lady entered. The sea-winds had been taking liberties with this young woman's hair, and it was blown in confusion all about the blue fore-and-after that she wore. Her dark blue mantle had the same wayward tendency, and her flannel blouse was confined at the neck by a most extraordinary tie of red. Though she walked with grace and modesty, she seemed to bring a breeziness into the room as soon as she entered. Even when she stood still and said nothing, she was so full of animal life that it made one eager for action simply to look at her. She looked so like the embodiment of the place, that I could hardly keep from addressing her as "Miss Tacoma." And imagine my astonishment at finding that this unconventional and frowsy young lady, with her imperious eyes, was the sister of my proper young friend—the daughter, in fact, to whom I had long ago refused to be introduced. I tried now to bring back some faint recollection of the state of mind that I must have been in to refuse a letter of introduction to a girl like this. I might have known Judge Curtis would have a nice girl. She had a little message to deliver

to her brother, who cast a prim look of dissatisfaction at the general reckless-
ness of her dress, and let her vanish without an introduction. That was how I
got punished for my churlishness back in St. Paul! But those things were in
the days when I thought I had a broken heart. After all, it might be that I
had only suffered a blessing in disguise.

There was life out here in the West, that was evident. If all had gone well
at home, I might still have been dully plodding in my office, ignorant of my
country, and hampered by a hundred traditions. Now, at least, I was out of
the rut, and I meant to stay out. And then, having arrived at this conclusion,
I tried to lead the conversation up to the amusement for the evening, in the
still nourished hope that I might be invited to spend it at the Curtis house. My
efforts, however, were not successful. We drove in the afternoon to Old
Tacoma, which was a hamlet when the new Tacoma lay hidden in blackberry
bushes and the unguessed future. The town has an interest of its own. The
modest houses nestle in among old trees, the gardens bloom, and everything
speaks of patient and quiet living; and quaintest of all is the little Episcopal
church, where—

> " More picturesque than chiseled stone,
>   But wrought by nature's hand alone,
>   A sylvan belfry stood.
>
> " A fir-tree's boll the shaft supplied,
>   And nestling quaintly by its side,
>   Behold the house of prayer;
>   No symbol these of power and pride,
>   But emblems of the Crucified."

Back again we drove, through a system of streets the existence of which I
had not suspected in my morning's walk, all well built, and giving evidence of
healthy growth.

"What would you have here, that you have not got?" apostrophized my new
friend, buttoning his immaculate driving-gloves, after we had taken a bottle of
California wine together, in one of the comfortable restaurants. "The coal
deposits of Puget Sound are the largest in the United States. This coal cokes
in the best sort of shape. You know the value of that, of course. The iron
deposits of the Cascade Range are enormous, and in time, with this coal adjacent, with the harbor at our very door, with a railroad that crosses half the
continent, we shall ship steel to all parts of the world. Do not look incredulous.
It is possible. It is probable. Another thing that you may not know, is that
the lime now worked on Puget Sound is the best on the Pacific Coast, and is
in itself an enormous source of wealth. I tell you, it is a place that a man may
be proud to work in. Stay here awhile, and you will agree with me."

But it was not alone to oblige my young friend, Dick Curtis, that I stayed in
Tacoma. For one thing, I was still waiting for him to ask me up to the house.
Meanwhile, I looked very thoroughly into the claims for commercial greatness
made by the city, and every day found myself growing in a desire to make this
place my home.

Tacoma, situated as she is, in the midst of the finest ship-timber in the West, is without doubt an embryo ship-building station. I spent several days in the lumbering regions, and returned to the city with the confirmed idea that better spars and keels never could be got out of any country.

The population of the town was estimated by the most modest at 30,000, but this is a low estimate. As a matter of fact, in a town under the present conditions of Tacoma, growing every day of the week, and every week of the year, it is next to impossible to rightly calculate the population, and an estimate that would be correct one month would be erroneous the next. Tacoma has four national banks, one private one, a savings bank, two steam-motor railways, several horse railways, a college and a seminary, public schools sufficient to accommodate the children, churches of all denominations, an elegant club house, one of the finest hotels in the United States—"The Tacoma"—several other comfortable hotels, and it is the headquarters for the Western Division of the Northern Pacific Railroad, that road having a fine general-office building, and repair and car shops there. New and much larger car shops are now under construction, which, together with the new tracks, will represent improvements, during the year 1890, to the extent of nearly $1,000,000.

I quote these facts to justify the enthusiasm which I felt over the town; for, in fact, I was delighted with the business of the place, and when I left it temporarily, to visit the State of Oregon, I did so under mental protest. Still, I wanted to do my duty by Portland and the Columbia.

The Northern Pacific carried me, in a few hours, to the compact city on the Willamette. Two things are noticeable in this town—the next in size to San Francisco, of the coast cities—first, the substantiality of the business blocks, and, second, the beauty of its residence sites. The streets are shaded with ash and maple, with horse-chestnut and elm trees; and, rising in luminous splendor to the skies, tower the mighty mountains of Jefferson, Hood, Adams, St. Helens, and Tacoma. As a great railroad center, Portland has advantages, united to those of being practically a sea-port, of which San Francisco has at times, so it is said, done the honor of being jealous. The Northern Pacific, the Oregon Railway & Navigation Co., and the Southern Pacific, all terminate here, and other local roads reach into the rich valleys of the State. I heard of the delights of the "Shasta Route"—otherwise the Southern Pacific—from a gentleman who had just reached Portland by that line; and he assured me that the journey was one continuous pleasure, passing, as he did, through the head of the Sacramento Valley, past the towns of Sisson and Edgewood, with the peerless Shasta in view, like some tender dream made visible; through Rogue River Valley, rich in gold and fruit; through the lands by the Umpqua and the Azalea rivers; through Eugene City, where the State University is situated; through Salem, a capital that reflects credit on its magnificent State; and then down that plenteous Valley of the Willamette, past Oregon City, to Portland.

The Valley of the Willamette, with its countless fruits, its prune farms,

LAKE KICHELOS, NEAR SUMMIT OF CASCADE RANGE.

which are a source of great wealth, its wonderful yield of grains—wheat, rye, barley, oats, and timothy—its wool-growing, and its mines—gold by streams and in quartz, copper, galena, and zinc—its dairying and timber, would form sufficient basis for a prosperous city on the site of Portland. But when it is taken into consideration that Portland is a manufacturing town of such extent that in the year 1889 her output of manufactured goods was no less than $20,000,000, her future can not be questioned. The climate at this point is so mild that the roses bloom till January, and the year round the landscape is beautiful. The population of Portland is no less than 50,000, and the coming census will doubtless show it to be more.

I took two short journeys during my stay in Portland. One was toward the mouth of the Columbia, to Astoria, which my great and enterprising townsman made famous. Here, built on wharves, I saw the historic town, which did not, in truth, wear a historic look, but which was brisk and bustling, and full of hopes for a great future. The great river—or rivers, for one now journeys on the Willamette and now on the Columbia—wore a look of tenderest beauty. The shores were lined with mighty trees, slender, straight, and eternally green.

" There grow the finest spars on the continent," said our captain, pointing to these shadowy forests, that stretched up beyond the beach over the misty hills. The islands that break the monotony of the land and fret the mighty current of the stream are said to be famous hunting-grounds, and, indeed, some of them are kept as preserves by the gentlemen of Portland.

My other journey was up the Columbia to the Dalles.

I felt aggrieved at having to take the steamer at 5 in the morning, but I summoned my fortitude, and reached the dock in the gray mist. I could see nothing but this blank wall of moist whiteness. It was dispiriting, to say the least; but I wrapped myself in my cloak, found a quiet place on deck, and sat shivering lest we should run into something. But suddenly, in the midst of this depression, a wonderful thing happened. I saw the whole curtain of mist become illuminated. It turned into a burning, billowing cloud of saffron, and then, like the uprolling of the curtain at a theatre, this glorified mist disappeared, mounting slowly, revealing first the shores, then the trees on the heights, then the far-off mountains, and finally the blue of heaven itself, as bright and as tender as the eye of a newly-awakened child. For the rest of the day there were no clouds. We passed, after twelve miles' ride, out of the Willamette into the green current of the Columbia. Pleasant pastures, rugged and fantastic heights, green and dewy dells, low nestling between the hills, and watered with crystal clear streams fed from the snows of the mountains, alternately delighted my eye.

Fort Vancouver, passed soon after entering the Columbia, is an important military post. Washougal is a town suggestive of prosperity and happiness in spite of its name. Beyond it lie many rocks which have, in the local nomenclature, names as commonplace as they are inappropriate, and I am not willing to lower this exquisite panorama by repeating them. They show a lack of invention, of knowledge of euphony and of poetry, as do too many other sections in my beloved America. Now a great shaft shoots presumptuously up toward the clouds, and haughtily sees its reflection in the swift green roll of the Columbia. Now a series of ambitious terraces, looking like the dismantled garden of some Babylonian palace, bewilder the eye with their intricacies. Now a rich prune orchard suggests the plenty of the fruitful valley, and again a bright flash of down-falling water shows where a mountain current breaks over the heights, to swell the seaward-bound flood. Shall I stab such beauty with daggers in the form of names like "Rooster Rock," and "Table Rock?"

At Warrendale is one of those extensive salmon canneries which have made so large a part of the wealth of this district. This is in the midst of the sternest scenery of the Columbia, where melancholy firs loom like hearse-plumes above the terrible grandeur of castellated precipices.

Not far beyond lies the "portage," but it bears no resemblance to the "portages" of early days, when the intrepid and muscular voyageurs packed their canoes on their backs and bore them beyond the cascades to more placid waters. Here it is the passengers who are carried, on a narrow-gauge railway, with the tumultuous cascades in sight, where the river once more resumes its calmer way. At one point the river is lost sight of, while the train rushes through a grove of fir. When once more the river breaks on the view, it lies far below in a rocky chasm, through which it frets and fumes in unavailing wrath. The Dalles—the old trading-post which bears no insignificant part in the history of Oregon—lies near the mouth of the Klickitat, and five miles beyond are the terrific Dalles of the Columbia, where the waters rise far above their normal height in forcing their mad way through the gorge.

I returned to Portland by rail, more to get a view of the Falls of Oneonta and Multnomah than for any other reason. The latter fall has a descent of 820 feet sheer down in two majestic leaps over a lichen and moss covered mountain-side. The "Pillars of Hercules" make an impressive break in the landscape; the river winds majestically in among the hills, and furnishes surprises enough to keep even the conventional tourist from wearying.

The annual State Fair was in progress when I returned to Portland, and I had the pleasure of visiting the neatest and most compact exposition building that I ever saw. Here were displayed those manufactures for which the town is distinguished, and the products of the rich lands adjacent to the Northern Pacific—Landreth wheat yielding from 40 to 60 bushels an acre; oats yielding from 75 to 100 bushels an acre; Chili Club wheat yielding 75; and timothy, barley, alfalfa of remarkable size and health. The only criticism I had to make upon the beautiful and thrifty town of Portland was the absence of any really elegant hotel; but I was consoled by the information that before another year had been ushered in, Portland would have one of the finest hotels in the world,

known as the Hotel Portland. The walls of this structure already arose impos-
ingly above the lesser buildings.

Hearing that I had missed much in the way of beautiful scenery by travers-
ing the road from Tacoma in the night, I determined to return in the day-time.
I found that I was fully repaid for this determination. We were taken across
the Columbia, at Kalama, on one of the largest transfer boats in the world, but
so quietly that I could with difficulty believe that the transfer was being made,
and I am sure that a good part of the passengers on this branch of the Northern Pacific never know that they have crossed the Columbia, unless they chance
to be assured of this fact by incontestable geographical evidence. We rode
through wild forests, beyond which rose, now and then, some dazzling peak
of snow.

Now, my Alaskan trip lay before me. Yet I was glad when I found that it
would be several days before the northern-bound steamer was due, and that I
could stay with a clear conscience in the "red town;" but the day for sailing
came at last, and in the early morning, while the great mountain lay flushing
under the morning sun, we sailed out of the harbor. The steamer carried
nearly her complement of passengers. I looked among them with curiosity,
not untempered with anxiety, to see if the companionship promised to be pleasant. It was all that could be desired—if one could judge by appearances—
and suddenly, with a start, I saw before me the young lady with the wind-blown
hair. Now I knew that I could make, in the most natural and friendly way,
the acquaintance of Miss Curtis.

And before night fell on those pleasant waters, I had done it.

There was a time when Alaska seemed more remote than Terra del Fuego,
and when the adventurer who returned from its shores was looked upon with
little less curiosity and admiration than that still accorded to an explorer from
Central Africa. And I myself thought of it as a tumultuous voyage, in which
I was likely to suffer not a little, until such time as I should get my sea-legs
on. Fancy, then, my relief at learning that our voyage would be almost entirely
inland, through the intricate island passages, and that only at four places should
we look out at the open Pacific. I learned, too, that the climate—which I
expected to find most bitter, and productive of great discomfort to the man
raised in temperate latitudes—was not so cold as much that I had become
accustomed to in my native city, the thermometer seldom reaching as low as
zero, even in midwinter, at Sitka. But I was assured by the officers that I had
done well to bring plenty of my warmest wearing apparel, because of the chilly
dampness that often accompanies the early morning and the evening. A
cautious investigation of the steamer convinced me that she was all I would
have, and that my apprehensions lest we should have a poorly appointed vessel
for this northern journey were entirely without foundation. I had come on the
steamer the night before, for the hour for sailing is at 4 in the morning, but
not being yet used to the idea of actually going to Alaska, I was up at the hour

PUGET SOUND FORESTS.

of sailing, and sat on deck while we made the three-hour journey to Seattle down the broad Sound. Port Townsend—"the Gate City of the Sound," as its people fondly call it—is the last American port touched at before entering British waters. Its population is about 5,000. To this are tributary the rich valleys of the Olympian Mountains. The Chimicum Valley is especially productive, the hops, grain, potatoes, and hay of that district commending themselves—so I was informed by a Port Townsend man—particularly to the buyers in town. All the shipping for Puget Sound is, of necessity, the shipping of Port Townsend, since every vessel entering the Sound is obliged to stop there. The town is, in fact, being benefited by the rapid development of the West, and property in its limits has doubled in the last three years. Several manufactories are now adding to the commercial prosperity of Port Townsend, and when to this is added easier access to the surrounding country, particularly to the iron deposits in the adjoining valleys, there will be no doubt of the future prosperity of this, the most northerly port of the west coast of the United States.

With Tacoma growing more cloud-like against the intense sky, and Mount Baker gradually brightening, we neared Victoria.

Quaint and calm is Victoria. The tourist knows it well, or at least every year Victoria knows more of the tourist. It looks out on a dainty, land-locked bay which reaches in from the Strait Juan de Fuca. The place has a fine equipoise, and is neither disturbed nor disturbing. Its beauties do not command—they implore—attention; and unless the visitor is inclined, he is not compelled to lift his eye above him, where the snow scintillates on the tops of the distant mountains; neither is he obliged to peer over the high fences into those exclusive English gardens for the pleasure of beholding flowers of tropical luxuriance; neither is he forced to take boat with the rest and row up to the gorge when the sun burns red in the west, and their rich banks gather to their dewy recess the shades of twilight; but he will do it if he stays, and if he has leisure he will certainly stay, for greater charms of mountain, stream, wood, and sea than Victoria has, whether for the sportsman, the artist, the idler or dreamer, are seldom found. Five miles distant lies Esquimalt, a British naval station, which is reached by a drive through woods thick with pine, spruce, arbutus, wild roses, and ferns. The dry-dock is a piece of masonry worthy the admiration of an American, who too seldom sees such things well executed in his own country.

We were given permission by our most obliging captain to disembark here for a few hours. The courteous young managing-editor of the *Colonist* was my guide through the town. He introduced me, among others, to John Fannug, hunter, taxidermist, and philosopher, who year by year swells the collection of native beasts and birds in the museum which stands among the other government buildings. These buildings, though not pretentious, are attractive and neat. The salmon furnishes one of the material sources of the financial growth of Victoria, 370,000 cases of salmon being shipped from the Fraser River alone, during the season of 1889.

And now, at last, I was started on my way to Alaska. That dim,
mysterious place about which I had so often dreamed was at last to become a
reality. Already I fancied the wind blew more sharply from the north, and
that the hills towering on each side gathered to themselves a sullen beauty, as
if the melancholy spirit of the northern seas floated down to them. A spasm of
homesickness came over me. But I had been sitting on the east side of the
deck, and now, to shake off the feeling of depression, I went to the other side.
What a contrast was here from that dun picture on which I had been looking!
Here was a glory of daffodil and azure in the west! The water responded with
a harmony of similar but softened tints. And there, in the forecastle, stood
Miss Curtis, wrapped in that enveloping mantle of blue, and frowning out at
the dazzling light in the west, like an amateur Hamlet.

It was then that I spoke to her. After that we took a mile turn on deck
after every meal, and sat for hours watching the slow passage of those sad hills
in their appealing beauty. She told me afterward that she felt quite safe in
chatting with me, without fear of misunderstanding, because her brother had
informed her that I was the victim of a hopeless passion, and much averse to
women. It was on this account that her brother refrained from introducing
us; he had supposed that it would be disagreeable to me! All this came
of my having told the Judge, back in St. Paul, that I did not care to know
women.

There are a few things that all Alaskan tourists appear to have in common.
These are fur rugs for the knees, novels of a mild sort, a furious desire to
collect curios, and a total ignorance of Alaskan affairs. The collecting of
curios began as early as Port Townsend, for there it was found the baskets of
the Cape Flattery Indians were superior to anything seen by anyone anywhere.
We all bought some, and asked each other the price of our respective purchases.
And from that time on, whenever a purchase was made on the voyage, even by
the most dignified member of the party, we all felt at liberty to ask what it cost,
and all the conditions of sale.

I can think of nothing more difficult than to try to systematize an account
of this Alaskan trip. Its delights lie to so great an extent in the unexpected,
and depend so much on the congeniality of the company, that I shall do justice
to it in no respect if I merely write the names of the places we passed and the
dull list of names of the places we visited. Fortunately, the vessel on which
we sailed carried a great deal of freight, and our stops at places of interest
were, therefore, longer than they otherwise would have been.

The days were never monotonous. There was always something new—
indeed, the whole thing was new. This succession of beautiful and dim
islands, of exhaustless mountains, of flashing waterfalls, this fascinating change
of tide and wind and sky, seemed to wrap us round with a sort of bewitchment
from which we would not willingly free ourselves, although conscious of our
thralldom. The visitor of the future, I am sure, will feel as we did, and, like us,

will care less for the names that these solitary bays and capes, these shadowy straits, lying between silent and untrodden mountains, may bear, than for the beauty that they display. However, lest the absence of names may vex some-one desirous of information, the usual course of the ship will be found below, not so free from mistakes, perhaps, but that the critical captains of the steam-ships may find fault with it, but as nearly correct as a person utterly ignorant of nautical matters and the navigation of the northern seas can make it.

After leaving Victoria, the steamer takes its way through the Gulf of Georgia, keeping Vancouver's Island on the west for 300 miles. Frequently, after passing through the archipelago, where islands lie in the blue liquid like jewels that crowd each other in some rich mosaic, the steamer stops at Nanaimo for coal. It then takes a northwesterly course, passing Taxada Island on the right. On this island is a large amount of iron ore, with a valuable percentage of phosphorus in its composition. Discovery Passage lies between Valdes and Vancouver's Island, where it winds tortuously between bluffs and headlands. The wider courses of Menzies Bay give way to Seymour Narrows, which bear a renown for hazard and for beauty. Even at low tide, the waters churn angrily here. At Chatham Point we amused ourselves by wondering how our vessel could pick out a road. When we were sure it would go to the right, it sud-denly turned to the left, and entered Johnston Strait.

It used to be a favorite amusement with us to sit on deck making wagers of one sort and another as to which channel the vessel would pass in the perplexing intricacy of ways before us. How narrow and dim these channels used to look from a distance, and how they used to widen and brighten as we entered them! The thread-like falls of water would flash down the emerald mount-ain-sides, the mists would seem to part to make way for us, till what a little while before had appeared to be a sea of shadows radiated with splendid colors and revealed vistas of luxurious greenness of coast and water, as warm and winning, I am sure, as anything that I should have seen had I taken that southern journey which my philosophic friend, the Frenchman, wished me to take. How I laughed now as I remembered the motive that brought me on this journey. Like the man who ceases to have the toothache as he approaches the dentist, so I had ceased to have the heartache as I prepared to take the remedy recommended by my friend—who certainly knew all about broken hearts, if any man did; for I never knew a man who had had so many.

But this is an inexcusable digression. I left off where we were riding through Johnston Strait—the white gulls wheeling round us, the fish leaping brightly in the water, the wind perfumed with balsamic scents—in the shade of the magnificent Prince of Wales range of mountains. The king of this tribe of mountains is the Albert Edward, on which the snows never entirely disappear, and which rises 6,968 feet above the sea. Thurlow and Hardwick islands are passed, and then the bay-indented shore of British Columbia is visible, and the ship enters the archipelago at the north of Johnston Strait. After this comes Broughton Strait, off from which shoots Alert Bay, with its salmon cannery.

"THE TACOMA."

Then entering Queen Charlotte Sound, and passing Fort Rupert, a Hudson's
Bay Company post, hastening for a brief time through Goletas Channel, with
islands to right, left, before, and after, we leave Vancouver's Island behind,
with its green Cape Commerell, and enter on that part of the Sound where the
Pacific sweeps into the mainland. Here, for a short time, it is the custom of
those of a retiring disposition to "seek the seclusion that the cabin grants."
But these are few, for the trials of the Sound are not great, and the wise sit on
deck and watch the long waves breaking on the distant shore, and the sun
plunging behind the purple curtains of the west, leaving behind an evanescent
mosaic of unnamed hues, to burn on the water. Mount Lemon looms on the
eastern horizon, meanwhile. Four brief hours bring the ship into Fitzhugh
Sound, under the shade of Calvert Island, where Mount Buxton towers. Passing the opening of Burke Canal, opposite the Hunter Islands, the steamer keeps
on a straight course till it suddenly swings into Lama Passage, which presents
something the shape of an open jack knife to the perplexed eye of the tourist.
And here, on Campbell Island, nestles Bella Bella, with its church spires and
its whitewashed cottages. This being the first sight of a native village, the
tourist usually expects something more peculiar than he sees in this neat and
inviting little village. It has such an air of cleanliness and prosperity that it
loses in picturesqueness.

"A certain amount of dirt and disorder is positively essential to picturesqueness," said Miss Curtis.

I could not help thinking, as I looked at her, that, although she was as
dainty as a "rose newly washed in the dew," she illustrated the proposition
to an extent; for she was never, by any circumstance, prim. I quoted to
her Herrick's lines concerning "a sweet disorder in the dress," and she seemed
to agree with his sentiments.

I could not help wishing that I had my acquaintance, the poet of Yakima,
with me as we entered Seaforth Channel, and I confess that I was impelled to
write a few verses myself, which, from motives of caution, I refrain from repro-
ducing. Here there are a hundred islands. Back of the pine and cedar clad
hills rise peaks of snow or rugged mountain-tops, bare and bitter. Over these
there hovers a pale gold haze, through which warm purple shadows play, till
the whole looks like some tremulous dreamland cheating the eye with its rich
fantasy.

At Millbank Sound we once more saw the Pacific, and a little later, paths of
ice marked the mountains with brilliant stripes of white, showing that we were
reaching those snows perennial with which the name Alaska is principally
associated in the mind of most persons. Finlayson Channel runs its narrow
way between the mainland and Princess Royal Island. The shores rise proudly
on each side to a height of 1,500 feet or more. Twenty-four miles brings the
ship into Wright Sound through McKay reach. Then comes the peculiar
Grenville Channel, which is as straight as a canal; then Arthur Passage, with

mountainous islands guarding it on both sides. Through the majestic Chatham Sound, by the side of the Chim-sy-an Peninsula, past Dundas Island and its towering caps of snow, we cross the line that furnished an ineffectual battle-cry to energetic patriots—" 54-40 or fight." We are, in short, at the dividing line between British America and Alaska.

" We are in Alaska!" cried Miss Curtis, dancing about on deck, and waving an anarchistical-looking scarf in the air.

" And the question is," said a political misanthrope, who felt the anomalous condition of the " district " in a most personal way, " What is Alaska?"

" I'll tell you what Alaska is," cried a citizen of Juneau, whom we were carrying back to his beloved camp; " it is the country for me. It has spoiled me for cities, and spoiled me for the States. I mean to stay up here, where I feel free. The wrongs of Alaska sound worse in Washington than they do here. We have what we want, and all sorts of legal recognition could not give us more."

But the pessimist shook his head. He felt that Alaska was suffering from great injustice, and he meant to suffer with her.

Still the question remained, " What is Alaska?" For one thing, Alaska is a country which, at the close of the year 1889, had compensated, by its revenue to the United States, for its purchase-money. In other words, the United States has taken as much money from that country as it spent in acquiring it. Alaska is a country with a coast line of 18,211 miles; its miles from east to west number 2,200, and from north to south 1,400. Its great river, the Yukon, is navigable for 2,000 miles. Its climate on the coast is equable and moist. In the interior, the heats of summer and the colds of winter are exceedingly great, although, perhaps, they are not more so than many other interior regions in which people live in contented civilization.

In the whole of Alaska there may be 3,000 white persons. There are certainly not more. The missionaries, the miners, the superintendents of the canneries, and the soldiers and sailors stationed at Sitka and interior points, make up this number. The number of native-born Alaskans approximates 34,000. Of these, the Aleuts, who are partly civilized, the Creoles, who are part Russian, the Innuits, the Thlinkets, and the Hydahs are, beyond doubt, of Oriental origin. Their physiognomies are essentially Japanese, and their traditions point to the fact of their having come from a country warmer than their own, and containing cities and great buildings. The Tinneh race alone is supposed to be Indian, and to have come from the interior. None of the Alaskans, however, are treated by the United States Government as Indians, and they suffer none of the disabilities of American Indians.

I am hardly willing to get ahead of my story by telling more of the Indians at this point. We became well acquainted with them and their habits before we left, and, perhaps, they can be best understood if introduced to the reader as they were to us. All along our journey, to the point at which we now were, the scene had been diversified by long bark canoes, filled with Indians, old and young, male and female, bound toward the south and the hop-fields of the Puyallup. Sometimes not less than forty were crowded into these skillfully maneuvered and gracefully built craft. Even the waters of Venice have not seen boats more graceful than these, fashioned by the natives of Alaska. The fore end of these boats has a bold upward sweep, not unlike that of a gondola, and often bears the figure of a fish or bird or beast carved on it with skill. With their bright turbans, their many-colored blankets, and their mysterious, dirty, but effective paraphernalia, these people presented an appearance most gratifying to the aesthetic eye, although it must be confessed that on close approach the perfume that emanated from the boats was not alluring.

"You ask what Alaska needs," Miss Curtis used to say. "No doubt our political philanthropist thinks it needs representation. I think it needs cologne." To tell the truth, both were right.

The riches of Alaska lie in its mines, its peltry, and its fish. Its vast tracts of timber look as if they might furnish fuel for the world. But on the coast the trees have not much commercial value, the trunks being covered with branches nearly to the ground, and the circumference being slight, although the height was goodly. Farther in the interior, however, it is said that the yellow cedar, a tree most valuable for ship-building, grows to a height of from thirty to forty feet before branching.

The development of the mineral wealth of Alaska is yet in its infancy. It may be as well at this point to give the results of such observations as I made, and which cover the more important mines of the country, with the exception of the placer mines of the Yukon.

The Treadwell mine, on Douglas Island, is the principal and most developed of Alaska mines. It is said that this mine pays its owners 100 per cent. a month. Certainly, there is gold enough in sight to excite even the experienced miner. The stamp-mill has 240 stamps, and its product is 600 tons of ore each twenty-four hours. The process by which the precious metal is extracted is said to give an average of 85 per cent. of the entire richness of the ore. To save the other 15 per cent. would demand a process more expensive than profitable when so great a profit is realized from the rougher treatment. This stamp-mill is the largest in the world, and ceases not its labors by day or night.

Adjoining the Treadwell mine is "The Bear's Nest," which was purchased by an English syndicate for a large sum. Its future is yet undecided. The popular impression has been that the lead of the Treadwell continued into this claim. East of and adjoining the Treadwell mine are those of the Eastern Alaska Mining and Milling Company, owned by Wisconsin men. This company has two claims, the "Mexico" and the "Belvidere," each 600 by 1,500 feet, and contiguous. A tunnel of 350 feet passes through 200 feet of milling rock of the same character as the Treadwell, of which the vein is a continuation. This company controls a stream which plunges down the mountain with sufficient velocity to run 800 stamps.

DEVIL'S THUMB, ALASKA

Behind Juneau rises a hill 3,000 feet in height, around whose base flows Gold Creek, a mountain stream having its rise amid glacial and snow mountains but a few miles distant. The stream runs through valleys and cañons whose soil is the washing of the hills, and is rich in precious metals. Along the hillsides and in the valleys are many placer mines. This canal by the stream is known by the name of "The Silver Bow Basin." The many mountain streamlets greatly facilitate operations in this valley. Here the "Takou Consolidated Company" has a ten-stamp mill, and the "Webster" has a five-stamp mill. Behind a large adjoining butte, a Boston company has a claim of sands, rich in gold, for which an outlet has been built into the valley below. These sands give the most immediate return for labor and outlay. At the head of the valley of the Silver Bow Basin stands the ten-stamp mill of the Gold Mountain Mining Company, which possesses a claim 600 by 4,670 feet in extent. The result of a ten-ton shipment from this mine gave $150 per ton. In close proximity to the stamp-mill is a water-power sufficient to run 200 stamps.

A mile and a half from the Silver Bow Basin is a parallel basin, in which have been discovered rich silver deposits. The "Silver Queen" lies near the top of a mountain, 1,300 feet above the beach. The shipments from this mine have been exceedingly rich. Were the mines of Juneau of less general interest to the public, an apology might be made for occupying space with specific information about them; but, without doubt, in Alaska lie the principal mining operations of the future. There are the gold and silver fields of the coming generations, and no information about them, however slight, can be amiss.

The seal fisheries, which bring to the Government over 4 per cent. on the money paid for Alaska, have been leased for twenty years—beginning with 1870—to the Alaska Commercial Company, which pays the Government an annual rental of $55,000 for the islands, and 2.62\frac{1}{2}$ each on the 100,000 seals which are annually killed, according to contract. The salmon fisheries of Alaska are increasing annually, and there are no less than fourteen extensive salmon-packing companies between Tongas Narrows and Juneau. At Killisnoo, on Admiralty Island, is the largest of the several whale fisheries. Herring and cod are also a large source of revenue.

Having given the reader some idea of the resources of this country, it may be well to briefly mention the condition of the missions now in existence, which he will be in a position to visit. It will be remembered that to the far north lie other missions, both Russian and American; but these do not so directly interest the tourist to Sitka, as he will have no opportunity of seeing them.

At Fort Wrangell there is a Government school and a Presbyterian church. The mission home for girls at Howcan has recently been burned, but will soon be rebuilt. Thirty girls are instructed at this school, and the church has a good attendance. At Douglas Island is a mission supported by the Friends Society. This is at present a home for girls; but, as the undertaking is in its infancy, it may in time become a more general institution. A night school is also in

6

existence. This is attended largely by the white miners, who attend in fort-nightly shifts—for, the Treadwell mine being worked by night as well as day, many of the miners have nocturnal duties.

At Juneau, a home is conducted in which there are twenty children. The utmost efforts are made here to establish friendly relations with the natives, especially among the women. The church accommodates 200 persons.

At Sitka are four schools—the Presbyterian mission, which is a training school, the Government school, a Catholic school, and a Russian school. Fourteen missionaries attend to the numerous departments of the training school, and the pupils number 150, of which forty-six are girls. The training school is also a home, and most of the boys and girls live under the roof, although a few in the village of Sitka return at night to their homes. The boys are instructed in carpentering, shoemaking, cabinet-making, blacksmithing, and, to a limited extent, in iron-work. In the future, when the necessary appli-ances are obtained, iron-work will probably become one of the established branches of mechanical instruction. The girls are taught all branches of domestic work and sewing. The part of the training devoted to letters is excellently sustained. Mr. Sheldon Jackson, for many years general agent of education in Alaska, presides over the school and the church at Sitka, and living, as he does, in the home with the pupils of the school, exercises a direct influence over them. Indeed, the habits of civilization are encouraged, even to the organization of a brass-band.

To guard against any danger of the pupils relapsing into their former barbarous state, Mr. Jackson has started a system of guardianship which follows the pupils after they leave the home. He encourages marriage between the pupils of marriageable age, compels the young men to make the furniture for a home before he will give his consent to their wedding, and advances money for them to build a house near the mission. The house and the ground on which it stands are then paid for by the young people in annual installments. And, in cultivating the arts of Christendom, the Indians have not been advised to lay aside or neglect the arts in which they naturally excel. They are, in many respects, artists of originality and skill—particularly those of the Hydah race. They are hereditary fishers and hunters. They can dress a skin well, make baskets and boats of great beauty and durability, and relate weird tales with a graphic brevity that distinguishes the stories of all primitive people who have had to rely upon tradition, instead of literature, for the preservation of their legends, their history, and their genealogical chronicles. None of these accomplishments are depreciated by the wiser of the Christian teachers.

Hospitals have been provided as an adjunct to the Sitka mission, in which all those taken ill, or suffering from any of the inherited diseases so prevalent among the Alaskans, are cared for by matrons who understand the particular needs of this class of patients.

The mission of William Duncan, the distinguished English missionary, is one of the most notable instances in the history of missions of the work that can be accomplished by one man. He and his 1,200 converts to Christianity having, as is well known, been forced to leave British Columbia, have settled on Annette Island, about sixty miles north of the southern boundary of Alaska, and named their habitation Metlakahtla, after the home they left with so much regret, and with a heroism that might as fittingly be sung of and preached about as the pilgrimage of the Puritan fathers. A church, far from rude, excellent homes, a good school, workshops, and all the evidences of a thriving village, are the result of the toil of the Indians in their new home. The systematic industry, the sense of honor, the growth and the demonstration of affection shown by these natives, is the result of the efforts of this one man, whose remarkable personality and sacrificial efforts will furnish one of the interesting chapters of the future history of the Northwest Coast.

This, then, was the country we were entering—a country of incongruities. At the Arctic Circle, yet not Arctic; a savage country, yet filled with Christian influence; a country supposed to be ice-bound, but in reality wrapped in perennial greenness; a frontier in which there is no warfare; a wilderness of scenic splendor, where one leaves the shelter of a glacier larger than the whole of Switzerland to bask in the sunshine of calm seas on which a summer mist lightly hovers.

As regards the agriculture of the country, there are various conflicting statements. Tubers are undoubtedly grown well, and the celery, the lettuce, the tomatoes, cabbage, turnips, and other table delicacies of a similar sort with which we were supplied on the boat, were from Alaskan gardens. Blue grass is being introduced on some of the islands, with a view to making pasturage sufficient to support cattle-ranches, and it is growing well. The coarse marshy grasses are liked very well by cattle, and, as these grow here in extensive quantities, the trial of cattle-raising is more likely to be a success. Wheat can be grown on many of the islands, but there is danger of early autumn rains, which prevent its being well cured. Nevertheless, the experiment has frequently been successful. It would, however, be inaccurate to say that it is not more hazardous than in the States and the wheat belt of British Columbia. But something of the surprises of the climate can be guessed at when I assure my readers that I never saw more exquisite roses than those growing in September at Sitka. They were such roses as we would have expected to have in New York State in June, but they had been in blossom from the early part of the summer, and were still full and stately and perfumed. By their side grew quantities of golden Californian poppies and beds of dark-eyed pansies, and chrysanthemums. The gardener will know by these flowers something of what can be grown in the vegetable bed. As yet, the experiments in agriculture in Alaska have been comparatively few. Certainly where mosses grow so high that one sinks in their exquisite carpet nearly to the knees, and where ferns grow till they resemble palm leaves in size, there must be encouragement for many sorts of useful vegetation.

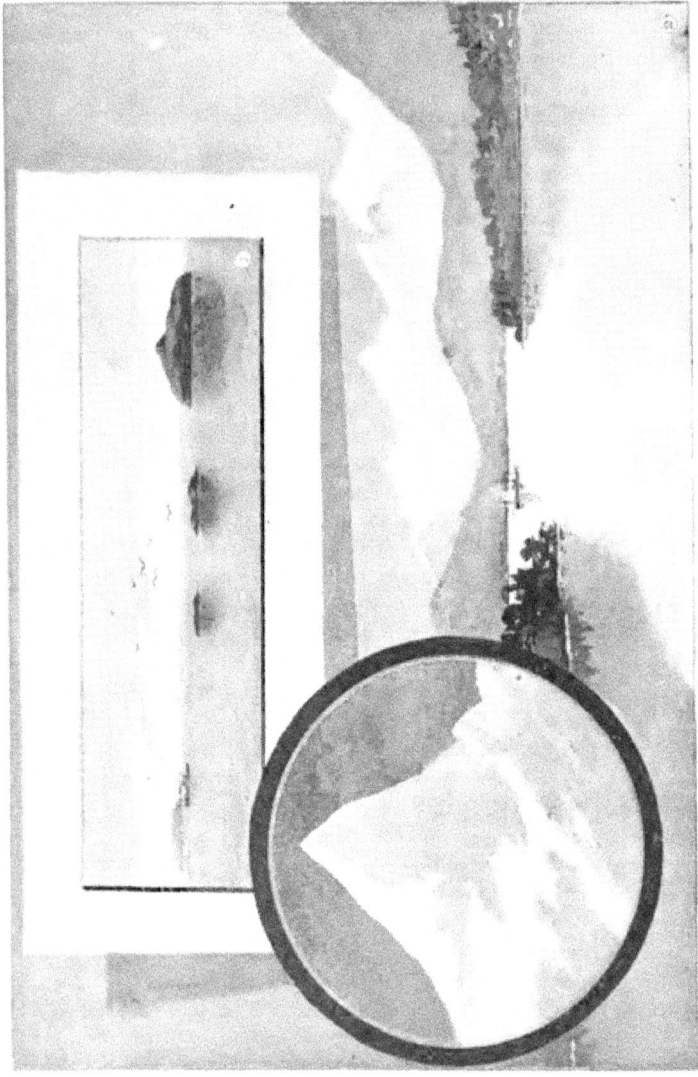

ALASKA—GATEWAY TO THE GLACIERS

1.—Millbank Sound.   2.—Stickeen Range.

Miss Curtis appeared to have an insatiable thirst for knowledge. She had a collection of books on Alaska which was truly formidable, and which she insisted on reading. Whenever we stopped at a landing, she made it a point to make the most systematic inquiries about the place, and as she enthusiastically related to me all of her most recently acquired knowledge, I was saved the trouble of putting myself out to any great extent in the accumulation of facts.

We saw the Pacific again at Dixon's entrance, and then entered Clarence Strait, which, with only a width of four miles, stretches ahead for over 100 miles. Close on each side crowd the hills, and in the waters at their feet they lie mirrored in translucent greenness.

But to return to our journey, and follow its course. The boat has performed its brief duties at Fort Simpson, which is the first American port after the British possessions, and when it stops at Tongas Narrows to deliver or take freight from the Tongas Salmon-Packing Company, it makes its second halt. The stop here is apt to be in the night, and, ten to one, the passenger does not know that he has an opportunity of putting his foot on Alaskan soil. But after he has really entered Clarence Strait, the good boat will steam into Loring, on Revilla Gigedo Island, some morning when a light mist is falling—at least, I fancy that the place must always look as it did when I saw it first.

Miss Curtis stood on deck clothed from head to foot in rubber.

"There are such advantages in being a man—or a mermaid," she said; "for then one can be more or less indifferent to the weather; as it is, I am bound to suffer. A woman is not only uncomfortable when it rains—she would not mind that so much—but she is a guy as well."

I and the "guy" went ashore together, by way of the long salmon-packing house, whose mysteries we made ourselves acquainted with. We had expected to experience some disgust; but we were agreeably surprised. The preparation of this familiar table luxury was as dainty as it could have been had it been prepared in a home kitchen. Nevertheless, there is something about seeing food in large quantities that is more or less disagreeable, and in the future we avoided the salmon-packing houses by common consent.

Beyond, in a sort of semi-circle following the beach, ran the little Indian village. Leaving the others to roam among these odoriferous dwellings in search of the treasured curios, Miss Curtis, two immature youths with long legs, and a charming and energetic young widow from Indiana, and myself, went in search of a waterfall whose noisy music, softened by intervening trees, came drowsily to our ears. The sand of the beach hardly ceases before the hill begins to rise. We passed a little garden, keeping always to the pipe that led from the cannery, and which ran directly to the fall, and presently entered the wood.

Suddenly the sun burst forth. The mist disappeared as if by the incantation of a magician; and there before us, in the most exquisitely harmonized tints of green and olive and brown, arose the wood, seemingly up to the very sky. From the branches of the firs trailed long festoons of moss, sometimes

deep in tint as the trees themselves, and again shading through fine gradations
of color till it shone yellow as a sunflower. Underneath was a dank carpet of
luxuriance. The mosses and the ferns, tangled in bewitching intricacy, rose half
to our knees, and bright berries of scarlet and crimson punctuated the greenness with points of vivid color.

"A Southern forest could not be more luxurious!" cried Miss Curtis, as she
paused, panting from her exertions, for the path, though not difficult, as mountain paths go, is far from easy. One climbs the slippery bulk of a fallen log
only to sink on the farther side into a mass of semi-peat made by the decaying
mosses and ferns of centuries; then up the boggy hill, plunges into deep-
tangled brush, or is obliged to swing by main force around the bulk of a tree,
whose outreaching roots make a strong barrier to progress.

"But," as Miss Curtis put it, "the difficulties make it more enjoyable. I
really felt afraid, when I saw how exceedingly comfortable my journey was
likely to be, that I should not have even the slightest feeling of adventure in
my Alaskan trip. I am positively grateful for the opportunity to show my metal
as a traveler, and to prove to myself that I am not a mere dining-car tourist.
It has always been a matter of regret to me that I was not a Columbus; but
even if I were a man, I am afraid I should be embarrassed by the fact that
there are no more worlds to discover."

This might have been a new world, however, for, though many hundred
had no doubt climbed, as we did, up this tangled slope, they had left few traces
of their presence, and we seemed to be moving in a forest previously unvisited
by man. Louder and louder grew the roar of the fall. There had recently
been a succession of heavy rains, and the stream had been swollen to a great
size. So, as we emerged from the thicket, and the tumbling mass of amber
water met our eyes, a cry of admiration burst from us—it was so much more
beautiful than anything we had anticipated. The surface of the rock over which
it plunged was broken with ledges and crossed with broken tree-trunks, so
that the swift body of water was whirled from it remorselessly, and, breaking
into a shower of yellow-tinted spray, flung itself angrily into the basin below,
where it seethed for a while, and then rushed on again between its glistening
mosses. Above the whole still rose the hill, draped to the very tops of the
ambitious trees with tender greens, which the sunlight revealed in all their surprising and varied loveliness.

I can not tell why it is that people always do absurd things in Alaska—and
I do not mean to insinuate that the residents do; but it is certain that the
tourists lose for a time that stern conventionality which binds them most of the
years of their life. In this picturesque wild, distinguished members of the
bench, senators, ministers, editors, artists, all of whom at home serve, no doubt,
as models of discreet conduct, here become boys, and frolic in a manner that
must be as surprising to themselves when they pause to contemplate it, as it is
to the witnesses; and the absolute relaxation that can be enjoyed is one of the

things that recommend this journey particularly to the man of exhausted brain.
There were no less than four gentlemen of wide public affairs on board with us,
all of whom were suffering from nervous prostration as the result of overwork.
At the close of the trip they owned to a decided improvement; I think they
would not have considered that they were perjuring themselves if they had said
that they were cured. The abuses and fatigues of years, however, can not be
made up for in one month's rest. But, undoubtedly, the ability to get away from
telegraph messages, from newspapers, from the reach of all business corre-
spondence, and the reports of all the happenings of this fevered age, is a
pleasure that few can appreciate the peace of till they have experienced it.
It seems like taking one month from the relentless passage of time, to grow
young in.

But I started out to say that we extracted more enjoyment from our walks
and explorations than can be conveyed by any description of our journey. If
we felt like using our lungs, we had actually lief to do so, and for some of us
who lived in cities the experiment was a novel one. We all wore rubber boots,
regardless of sex, and the fording of streams, the wading in the surf, the climbing of mountains, and the leaping of logs filled us with no dismay.

Fatigued, but not exhausted, by the exploits at the fall, we rowed, in the late
afternoon, through a narrow inlet to where a silver lake lies among the mountains, like a pearl in a cluster of emeralds. The shores are wild and luxuriant,
and the very "cave where echo lies" seems to be here.

Fort Wrangell was our next stopping-place. This was once the port for the
Cassiar mines, and, as such, a place of importance. But now it is a small
trading-post with a few Americans living among the Indians. Stikine River
Indians occupy the huts that circle around the beautiful sweep of beach. We
went out on shore as soon as the gang-plank was swung out. The town was
more representative than the one we had previously visited. It is noted for a
number of remarkable totem-poles and old Indian graves. The totem-pole, as
is now generally known, is a genealogical chronicle, represented by carvings.
The races having tribal division, named after the raven, the whale, the frog, the
eagle, and, possibly, the blackfish, signify the marriages by the succession of
figures carved on these poles. It would be interesting to devote a short chapter
to the habits of the Indians, and particularly upon their tribal relations and
government, as well as their not unpoetic superstitions and traditions, did space
permit. But so many readable volumes have recently been written about the
Alaskans, that, without doubt, most tourists start upon their journey with some
acquaintance with the subject. At Fort Wrangell we visited these totem-poles,
following a road past the main part of the town to a sequestered little peninsula, where a second group rewarded our exertions. I remember, too, that I
spurred Miss Curtis on to a tour of investigation, and going back of the houses
near which these totems stand, came upon a remarkable scene. An Indian hut,
somewhat more moss-covered than the others, overlooked the bay, and about

the door clustered a group of those sharp-featured and contemptible coyote dogs, whose cowardly natures irritate a lover of "Christian dogs," as we referred to those of the States. In the dim light of waning day the interior of the hut was visible to us by the blaze of the fire which was built on the ground in the center of the house, and around which the family were clustered. The house was terraced, or erected in platforms; that is, after climbing several steps to gain entrance to the door, one is obliged to descend two or three platforms which run around the entire house, to reach the ground. The family utilize these platforms for beds, tables, seats, store-houses, and display-shelves. Indeed, this style of architecture seems so well suited to their needs that I could not help admiring it. In the place of honor, exactly opposite the door, sat the head of the house. Near him sat his wife, his sons and his daughters. With their backs to the door were two more dejected mortals, whom we took for slaves, and all about among the group were cats of formidable size and the most sociable habits. It was the first time that we had chanced upon an Indian family in the full enjoyment of their domestic happiness, and the picture made a strong impression. The house was soaked with moisture, being very old and moss-covered. The dogs kept up a mournful and wolfish howling, and the cats blinked solemnly at those silent and old-faced children.

Filled with a sudden appetite for the curious, we retraced our steps for a short way, and then picked our way across a narrow and quaking bridge to a lonely island surrounded by tide-lands. Here stands the house of the chief, who is the proud possessor of many of the best pieces of work ever done by his tribe. Here are more totems, both inside and outside, and there is besides a most amazing conglomeration of Catholic emblems, heathen carvings, Chinese chests, Russian furniture, Indian blankets, and American clothes, that I ever saw.

We delayed our visit to the old stockade and block-house and the Government buildings till morning. The little plaza in front of them was green and inviting. The port-holes, yawning through the walls of the old fort buildings, looked innocent enough under the light of existing circumstances, and it took all of our imagination to summon up pictures of desperate struggles with the Indians, such as took place here in other days. But the morning was not far advanced when we were on our way. Never shall I forget through what tortuous narrows we then made our way; nor how the gulls wheeled and wheeled about us with their deafening din; nor how the red and black buoys marked the course of the ship. The Jumbo Mountains towered in the distance, and at a certain turn we came in sight of the Fairweather range. How shall I tell how beautiful those peaks of snow looked, poised against the sky with the changeful loveliness of clouds? Mount Fairweather, 13,500 feet; Mount Crillon, 15,900 feet; Mount La Perouse, 11,300 feet; Mount Lituya, 10,000 feet, shine together, far, far to the north. We were especially fortunate in being able to see them at this distance, so we were told; but for us the day was perfect. To be sure, the wind blew cold; but Miss Curtis sat wrapped, with the dear little widow from Indiana, in voluminous wraps, on the forecastle, and I, with my legs in a coil of rope and my shoulders covered with a series of capes, kept safe from danger of chill. The scene changed every moment, and we must have been much colder than we were to have sacrificed any of its beauties.

If geographical terms are to be continued, it may be mentioned that after going westward to the southern entrance of Wrangell Strait, the ship goes northward into Dry Strait, on the right of which is the Patterson glacier. Dim and distant does it look, however, and one receives no hint from this view of the peculiar and transcendent splendor of the glaciers when seen at close range. The serpentine streams of ice crawling down the mountain-sides to the ocean became more frequent as we still sailed to the north, and we are not surprised now to encounter cakes of floating ice. Kupreanoff Island, Frederick Sound, and Stephen's Passage passed, we hastened on till we reached Taku Inlet. It is not the habit of the vessels to put in here on every voyage, but on this particular occasion, a United States Survey ship wanting coal, anchor was weighed at the little settlement. The place would not have lingered in my memory, but for a peculiar circumstance. So perfect was the night—moonlight, with pale stars—that I could not persuade myself to go to bed, but sat on the upper deck, thinking of—well, of many things. I was lying back on the tightly drawn canvas that covers one of the small boats, when I was electrified by seeing an arm of crimson radiance dart into the sky to the very zenith, while after it came rolling, as from an invisible horn, a liquid illumination, white and shimmering. A second later, the whole northern sky was alight with weird, green shadows, with those wavering pennons of red and those ghostly wings of white. It was the aurora borealis. I had supposed that I had witnessed this phenomenon many times in my life, but I knew now that what I had previously seen was but the faintest shadow of the reality. Faster and faster played this wild dance of prismatic gleams, reaching down into the atmosphere till it seemed to play among the rigging of the ship, and filled me with something like fear. It was so capricious, so mystical, that I feared it would wrap me round and envelop me in some strange enchantment. My growing terror was increased by the sight, at the far end of the deck, of a white figure, that seemed to flutter and hover in the very midst of this bewitchment. This figure at last glided toward me, and I saw that it was Miss Curtis, wrapped in a huge eider-down mantle. She had a sort of uncanny look in her eyes, and I can not say that my awe was lessened by finding that she was no ghost. Seating herself on the edge of one of the small boats, and throwing back her head, so as not to lose one transformation of this impressive spectacle, she began reciting one of Longfellow's adaptations of the Icelandic skaulds. This finished, we " fell on silence " till slowly the splendor in the sky vanished and left the quiet and familiar moon; then, without a " good-night," she glided off again, and left me to a disturbed solitude.

The next day, I could not find even a moment's opportunity of seeing this young lady, who seemed to have caught an erratic spirit from the wild luminosity in which she had bathed herself the night before. She cultivated old gentlemen, and invalid ladies, and the Indians in the forecastle—anyone but me. Not till we reached Juneau did I again have an opportunity of speaking more than a sentence with her.

Juneau lies on the beach at the foot of precipitous hills. Its population is not less than 1,500, the greater part of which is native. However, there are many American men here, interested in the mines, and there is that famous

ALASKA—STEAMER IN ICE FIELD.

character, Dick Willoughby. Dick Willoughby is the typical pioneer; dressed in blue-jeans, with the swagger of the mountaineer and the arm of a boatman, he can give more information, in his not irreproachable English, concerning Alaska, than a dozen other men. He is intrepid, strong in spite of advancing years, the best of companions, and one of the most indefatigable of explorers. That he is imaginative, some persons believe who have not seen the "Silent City," that famous mirage which he claims to have discovered on the Muir Glacier; but, certain it is, that every recurring midsummer season for many years Mr. Willoughby has gone upon a long and mysterious pilgrimage, which he now says has always been to the site of the city in the air. At present, scientists disclaim the possibility of the existence of such a mirage; but the scientists have so often been wrong in their premises, and false in their conclusions, that it will be as well to delay judgment in this matter till later investigations have conclusively proved these interesting tales to be false.

At Juneau, by the courtesy of the owners of the Gold Mountain mine, I was taken to the terminus of the road constructed through the Silver Bow Basin—the only road of any length in Alaska. The cañon was very like Colorado in many of its features, so I was informed by a gentleman from that State. It was certainly a proud picture, with its rugged sides, its snow-covered barricades at the far end; its flashing rivers, and dells where the ferns and brushes grow. There are some pleasant homes at Juneau, and a few shops which would be no disgrace to a town in the States; but this last is true of all of the trading-posts, Fort Wrangell having several excellent stores. Here, too, are some good curio stores ; but I was assured by the ladies that, though one could frequently find some desirable bit of Hydah carving or silverwork in the shops, quite as often the most desirable curiosities were got from the Indian houses. One native silversmith at Fort Wrangell met with especial recommendation for the characteristic work he did, while the rattles, the totems, the beads, fish-hooks, and furs of Koehler & James, at Juneau, were said to be worthy of particular examination. Juneau is perhaps the best place to buy furs, there being several good dressers of furs at that place, and the country round about being favorable for the trapping of many of the best fur-bearing animals. Juneau has two weekly papers, which the tourist reads with interest, and which keep the residents fairly well informed of the affairs of the Territory, especially among the mines.

We made our way northward through the Lynn Canal. On the sides of the barren mountains gleam the glaciers. Vegetation almost ceases. Eagle Glacier is seen after passing Point Retreat, and the mighty Davidson is passed soon after. Then come the inlets of the Chilkat and Chilkoot, barren and grim, with the wind blowing cold from fields of ice, and nineteen cataracts from these frozen stretches flowing fiercely into the sea. Pyramid Harbor is the point at which the vessel stops longest in these inlets. It takes its name from a symmetrical rock which rises in solitary desolateness in the midst of the ever-altering tides. Is is worth while to go ashore here and walk for a mile or two. One will not arrive anywhere in particular; but the tourist will see before him a mountain of glittering ice that increases in beauty as he keeps on his way. I returned to the ship to find everything ready for departure.

I stood by the bulwarks, deep in thought, when Miss Curtis passed—and spoke.

"You look as if you had just made up your mind to sacrifice yourself for the good of mankind," she said, archly.

" I have made up my mind," I said, "that if a man wants to be happy, he can not do better than to live here among these ingenuous savages. Here, with wastes of ice and snow, these solemn rocks and terrible rivers surrounding one, it might be possible to cultivate a high and serious train of thought. I am wondering if it is worth while to return to civilization. There, one's best motives are misconstrued; one is constantly put to it to get bread to keep life in his body. Every man is against his fellow, and the end of all is disaster —death—forgetfulness."

" Yes," replied Miss Curtis, wrapping and rewrapping a scarf about her neck, with a graceful twining of her arms, " I should think you might enjoy staying here and assisting in the manufacture of those Chilkat blankets, one of which I have just purchased for sixty good dollars, and which I expect to decorate the side of my sitting-room with, when I can get the smell out of it."

" I do not admire the famous Chilkat blankets," I said, testily, " and I wonder how it is that you always refuse to understand and respond to my moods, when you find it so easy to sympathize with others."

There was no reply to this, and I went on:

" To-morrow we shall be at the Muir Glacier, and I think of leaving the vessel, hiring a canoe of natives with whom I have already spoken at Chilkat, and exploring the icy fastnesses of that region."

" If you really want to commit suicide," said the lady, angrily, " why not do it in some quicker way?"

" I wish to be alone," I replied, still preserving what I supposed to be a dignified and impressive demeanor; " and surely there I shall be so; my fate will trouble no one."

" I thought you said you were going to become one of the devoted citizens of Tacoma?" interposed my saucy girl.

" Why should I stay where I am not wanted?" I burst forth.

" I am sure the legal profession needs you," was the answer I got.

I drew myself up haughtily.

" I shall leave you at the glacier," I said. I expected that this would touch a woman, but it only had the effect of producing a ribald peal of laughter.

" Pardon me," I said, " I am glad you can laugh, but I do not feel called on to furnish you any more amusement." I lifted my hat. I started to walk away. The laughing stopped.

" I suppose you have no objection to a companion on the glacier," said a very gentle voice. I returned and looked at the speaker. She was winding and unwinding that scarf again.

" You have treated me shamefully the last few days," I cried, taking no notice of her last remark. There was no answer.

" Now, I suppose," I went on, " you wish to make a fool of me. You are going to lead me on by remarks such as you just made to heights of hope from which you will suddenly dash me."

" Oh, very well," cried she, " if you wish to misunderstand me. I suppose you like to be miserable—that is, if you really are miserable. Perhaps you are only pretending."

" Do not be angry," I cried; " you can guy me all you like, but do not avoid me as you have been doing. If I really went on the glacier, would you go?"

" I think I might," she said, laughingly. Then she pretended that someone was calling from the after cabin, and started to hasten toward it.

" But if I stay in Tacoma—which, I must say, is the town of my heart's election—may I feel that you take an interest in my success?"

"Why certainly," she called, still hastening on. I caught at that voluminous scarf.

"Let us have no more evasion," I pleaded. "I will stay and carve out my fortune there, if you will promise me that I shall have a home there." Some one was approaching. She feigned to be laughing.

"Then come up and keep bachelor's hall with my brother," she said.

"Not bachelor's hall," I objected.

"Oh, very well; as you like," she replied.

"Is it a promise?" I asked, hardly daring to believe she meant it.

"It is a promise," she said suddenly, ceasing to laugh. Then a dozen people came along, and we fell to talking about the atmospheric effects.

The next day—or rather in the light of the early northern morning—we entered Glacier Bay. First we sailed through quantities of drifting ice, the ship now and then staggering from the concussions with it, and the Captain unable to conceal a certain nervousness.

"This is the heaviest fall of ice from the glacier that I have seen in years," he confided to me. But the ship went on, slowly picking its way. I stood on the forecastle with my lady; both of us were wrapped from head to foot in our recently-purchased furs. The day was perfect, and the vision uninterrupted for miles.

The sea was a brooding blue; the sky a blue of deeper tint. The mountains were wrapped in mists of blue, and the tremulous air seemed a liquid sapphire diluted with some tender and ethereal radiance. The cakes of ice floating about the veering ship were white, with crevices of ultramarine. These groaned and swayed with the contesting tides, for the glacial stream combated with the rising waters of the incoming tide, and the perplexed bergs were the victims of the struggle. In the sky two copper-colored orbs burned through the luminous ether, and so bright was the mock sun that it required a second and searching look to determine which was the real sun, and which its reflex. Thus, by the mystic light of two suns, the trembling vessel forced its way through the clustering bergs to where the engulfing blueness seemed to concentrate itself into an intensity deeper than any mid-summer sky, more radiant than my lady's eyes, more brilliant than any sapphire, more splendid than any tint of wave in sunlit depths. We stayed at the glacier for twelve hours. We climbed past its great moraine and looked into its scintillant crevasses. We learned of colors, the existence of which the imagination could not dream. But while the rest chatted and exclaimed, I and one little lady kept silent. It seemed but natural and right that such a scene of glory should emphasize our happiness. The roar of the falling ice, as it dropped into the protesting sea, was the orchestral accompaniment for life's melody.

Southward next, through Chatham Strait, into the placid Peril Straits, which belie their name, in sight, in course of time, of the blasted crater of Edgecumbe, and we enter the harbor of Sitka. Innumerable islands dot the bay; in the west rises the Mount of the Holy Cross, with its sacred sign of unsullied snow; and on the pier stand the groups of fantastically dressed Indians, the navy officers, and their wives, a delegation from the mission, and a few lads bearing the costume of the United States men-of-war. Green and smooth is the well-kept plaza or parade ground, and beyond it is the graceful Greek church, and the quaint Russian houses, with their whitewashed walls, and their gardens, while round the beach stretches the Indian village in picturesque irregularity.

How to crowd all of our sight-seeing into twenty-four brief hours puzzled us. We visited the stores, accumulated more curios, dined at the excellent inn kept by Mr. Milmore, and washed in the room where Lady Franklin slept, on her weary search. Grouse and venison, native cranberries, and delicious native-grown vegetables, made up a dinner that none of us are likely to forget, any more than we are the walk that preceded it, and which added materially to the appetites with which we astonished " Dazzle," the diminutive waiter at the " Milmore." This walk was to the last battle-ground of the Thlinkets, over roads of crushed stone, through a wonderful forest. Here the intermingling boughs made a canopy, and balsamic perfumes greeted the nostrils. The ferns and mosses carpeted the ground, and the thicket reached up to the heights above in almost impenetrable luxuriance. Indian River bubbled and swirled over its innumerable stones, sending its crystal current to mingle with the silver waters of the bay. Another road took us to the "big trees," where mighty cedars have grown from the stumps of decayed trees, producing a most peculiar effect. Sometimes we crossed rustic bridges, over whose slippery surface my lady needed assistance; sometimes we leaped from root to root amid dank paths of rotten fern; sometimes we stopped to admire the flow of the river, in which we could see the fish leaping.

And after dinner we went to Baranoff Castle. The light lingers so late that we had no fear of the ghostly lady, who, murdered in the ball-room on her bridal night, still haunts these deserted halls to remind mortals of her tragic fate. So we climbed the rotting stairs to the old mansion, built of wood, on solid rock, which, when the site was an island, made a natural fortress which assailants might have had much difficulty in carrying. The red light flushed all the bay, and by it we saw by what allurements the great captain and statesman, Baranoff, was brought to make his settlement at this spot.

The next day we visited the training school, receiving many courtesies from the missionaries, and the Greek church, which is a bit of a richer civilization dropped down into this severe atmosphere. Its pictures, vestments, jewels, and censors are in strongest contrast to the simple white missions farther along the shore, but they both represent an influence more similar in its results than the followers of either faith would be likely to admit.

I wanted to journey to the head of Silver Bay, and see the Sarabinokoff Cataract; to climb the sides of Edgecumbe, and visit the deer-haunted fast-nesses of Vostovia; but, under the circumstances, I was willing to leave this interesting and historic city—for was not my lady with me? To be sure, the glimpse I had of one delightful interior of an old Russian house, and of the heirlooms that enriched it, made me long to stay in an atmosphere so full of reminiscences. But as I neared the steamer the half-hour before we lifted anchor, and its familiar decks hove in sight, I felt only a desire for a continuation of the journey through this land of mellow twilights, of eternal silence, and slumberous reaches of shadowy seas.

Our journey home was broken by several stops. The days came to be treasured more and more as the time for leaving our good ship drew near. We had made friends on board with whom we were loth to part. And over these friendships was thrown a glamor of the unusual and the romantic which will forever make them distinct. Stronger, happier, more appreciative than ever before of home comforts, we returned to Tacoma.

Our experience in these majestic channels, surrounded with a succession of inimitable scenes, was one not to be forgotten so long as memory holds power to summon at will the pleasures of the past.

As for me—there is Tacoma, the city of destiny, and the lady of my love!

NORTHERN PACIFIC R. R.

Rates and Arrangements for the Tourist Season.

MINNESOTA SUMMER RESORTS.—The Northern Pacific Railroad will sell round-trip excursion tickets from St. Paul or Minneapolis to Glenwood (Lake Minnewaska) at $5.25; Battle Lake, $7.50; Fergus Falls, $7.50; Detroit Lake, $9.15; Minnewaukan (Devil's Lake), $18.65; Winnipeg, $22.50. From Duluth or Superior to Battle Lake, $7.50; Fergus Falls, $7.50; Detroit Lake, $9.15; Minnewaukan, $18.65; Winnipeg, $22.50. From Ashland, Wis., to Battle Lake, $9.00; Fergus Falls, $9.00; Detroit Lake, $10.65; Minnewaukan, $20.15; Winnipeg, $22.50. Tickets on sale May 1st to September 30th, inclusive. Good going to Minnesota resorts one day (from Ashland two days), to Minnewaukan (Devil's Lake) and Winnipeg two days from date of sale. Good to return on or before October 31st.

YELLOWSTONE PARK RATES.—The Northern Pacific Railroad, the only rail line to the Park, will sell round-trip excursion tickets from May 30th to September 25th (both dates inclusive) at the following rates.

A $110.00 Book Ticket, including the following traveling expenses, from St. Paul, Minneapolis, Duluth or Ashland on the east, and Portland or Tacoma on the west, to and through the Park and return to starting point, viz.: Railroad and stage transportation, Pullman sleeping car fares, meals on Northern Pacific dining cars and at Hotel Albemarle at Livingston (junction of Main Line and Park Branch), and board and lodging at the Park Association Hotels five and one-quarter days.

A $50.00 Round-trip Ticket, St. Paul, Minneapolis, Duluth or Ashland to Livingston and return.

A $12.50 Book Ticket, Livingston to Mammoth Hot Springs Hotel and return, including rail and stage transportation and one and one-quarter days' board at Mammoth Hot Springs.

A $35.00 Book Ticket, Livingston to Mammoth Hot Springs, Norris, Lower and Upper Geyser Basins and return, including rail and stage transportation, and four and one-quarter days' board and lodging at the Association Hotels.

A $40.00 Book Ticket, Livingston to Mammoth Hot Springs, Norris, Lower and Upper Geyser Basins, and Yellowstone Falls and Cañon and return, including rail and stage transportation and five and one-quarter days' board and lodging at the Association Hotels.

Limit and Conditions of Tickets.—The $110.00 Ticket will be on sale at eastern and western termini named, May 30th to September 27th, inclusive; by eastern lines, May 29th to September 26th, limit 40 days; good going 30 days, returning 10 days, but must be used in the Park before October 5th. Stop-overs within final limit at or east of Billings, and at or west of Helena. Return portion of ticket must be signed and stamped at Mammoth Hot Springs Hotel, after which ticket must be presented on Main Line train for return passage within one day from such date. Stop-overs in Park granted at pleasure of holder within final limit of ticket.

Limit of $50.00 Ticket and stop-over privileges same as above, return portion of ticket to be stamped and signed at Livingston ticket office.

Coupons in Book Tickets may be used in Park without regard to items or localities specified on their face.

The $12.50, $35.00, and $40.00 Tickets, on sale at Livingston and eastern and western termini between dates first named above, are good if used in the Park any time between June 1st and October 1st, both dates inclusive, and do not require identification of purchaser.

IMPROVED HOTEL ACCOMMODATIONS.—A new and commodious hotel at the Grand Cañon, with accommodations for 300 guests, will be opened to the public June 1st, thus enabling tourists to remain at this, the chief point of interest in the Park, as long as may suit their convenience and pleasure.

A DAILY STAGE LINE.—The Transportation Company will run a daily line of stages during the entire season, in both directions, between the following points, i. e., Cinnabar, the terminus of the Northern Pacific's Yellowstone Park branch, and Mammoth Hot Springs, a distance of seven miles; Mammoth Hot Springs and Upper Geyser Basin, via Norris, Lower and Midway Geyser Basins; Norris Geyser Basin and Yellowstone Lake, via the Grand Cañon.

NO CHARGE FOR STOP-OVER PRIVILEGES IN THE PARK.—This daily stage line will be operated solely for the benefit of tourists who may wish to stop off at any point of interest longer than the time allotted in the schedules. Where tourists stopping over desire the carriage in which they are making the trip detained, an extra charge will be made. For time schedules and prices, see "Wonderland Junior."

HOTEL AT YELLOWSTONE LAKE.—A small hotel, with capacity to accommodate about 100 people, is being erected on Yellowstone Lake, near the outlet, and will be ready for guests early in the season. This point may be visited, at the option of the tourist, from the Grand Cañon. Stage fare Grand Cañon to the Lake and return, $6.00. A steamboat, with accommodations for 150 people, will make a daily excursion from the hotel on the Lake, covering a distance of about 100 miles. Fare for round trip, $5.00.

MONTANA AND EASTERN WASHINGTON POINTS.—The Northern Pacific Railroad sells daily round-trip excursion tickets to Bozeman at $52.00; Helena and Butte, $56.00; Missoula, $62.50; and Spokane Falls at $70.00.

These tickets will be of iron-clad signature form; will require identification of purchaser at return starting point, and will be limited to 90 days, good going 30 days and returning 30 days. Stop-overs granted at any point within limits stated.

To Springdale (Hunter's Hot Springs), Mont., and return, $50.00; on sale daily; good 40 days—going limit 30 days, return limit 10 days.

NORTH PACIFIC COAST EXCURSIONS.—An $80.00 Round trip Individual Excursion Ticket, St. Paul, Minneapolis, Duluth or Ashland to Tacoma, Portland, Seattle or Victoria, is on sale daily at points first named and by eastern lines.

Tacoma, Seattle, Victoria or Portland tickets at above rates will be *issued*, going via Cascade Division, returning via Columbia River Line, or vice versa; Portland tickets via either Cascade Division or Columbia River, returning via Union Pacific to either Omaha or Kansas City, and Victoria tickets good to return via Canadian Pacific to either Winnipeg, Pt. Arthur, St. Paul or Minneapolis.

CONDITIONS.—Above tickets limited to six months from date of sale; good going trip 60 days to any one of North Pacific Coast termini named, returning any time within final limit.

ALASKA EXCURSIONS.—An excursion ticket will be sold from eastern termini named to Sitka, Alaska, at $175.00, which rate includes meals and berths on the steamer. Tickets on sale May 1st to September 30th. Limit, six months. Going to Tacoma, 60 days, returning within final limit, holder to leave Sitka on or before October 31st. Usual stop-over privileges granted. Steamer accommodations can be secured in advance by application to any of the agents named below. Diagrams of steamers at office of General Passenger Agent at St. Paul.

CALIFORNIA EXCURSION RATES.—The Northern Pacific Railroad will sell round-trip excursion tickets from St. Paul, Minneapolis, Duluth or Ashland, via Cascade Division or Columbia River and Portland, and either the Shasta route or the ocean to San Francisco, returning same route, or by southern lines to Omaha, Kansas City, Mineola, or Houston at $95.00; to New Orleans and St. Louis at $101.00; to St. Paul or Minneapolis via Missouri River, $105.00. Tickets via ocean include meals and berths on steamer.

At the eastern termini of the southern transcontinental lines, excursion tickets will be sold, or orders exchanged, for tickets to San Francisco, returning via either the Shasta route, the all-rail line to Portland, or the ocean and the Northern Pacific to St. Paul, Minneapolis, Duluth or Ashland, at rate $15.00 higher than the current excursion rate in effect between Missouri River points, Mineola or Houston and San Francisco. The steamship coupon includes first-class cabin passage and meals between San Francisco and Portland.

Return coupons reading from Missouri River points to Chicago or St. Louis will be honored from St. Paul or Minneapolis, either free, or with a small additional charge, according to the route.

These excursion tickets allow six months' time for the round trip; 60 days allowed for westbound trip up to first Pacific Coast common point; return any time within final limit.

General and Special Agents.

- A. D. CHARLTON, Assistant General Passenger Agent, 121 First St., Portland, Ore.
- JAMES C. POND, Assistant General Ticket Agent, St. Paul, Minn.
- B. N. AUSTIN, Assistant General Passenger Agent, St. Paul, Minn.
- J. L. HARRIS, New England Agent, 306 Washington Street, Boston, Mass.
- E. R. WADSWORTH, General Agent, 210 South Clark Street, Chicago, Ill.
- GEO. R. FITCH, General Eastern Agent, 319 Broadway, New York City, N. Y.
- C. B. KINNAN, Eastern Passenger Agent, 319 Broadway, New York City, N. Y.
- A. D. EDGAR, General Agent, corner Main and Grand Streets, Helena, Mont.
- JAMES McCAIG, General Agent, 354 Main Street, Butte, Mont.
- A. W. HARTMAN, General Agent, Duluth, Minn.
- H. SWINFORD, General Agent, 457 Main Street, Winnipeg, Manitoba.
- A. ROEDELHEIMER, General Agent, corner High and Chestnut Streets, Columbus, O.
- G. G. CHANDLER, General Agent, 621 Pacific Avenue, Tacoma, Wash.

Traveling Passenger Agents.

- A. J. QUIN, 306 Washington Street, Boston, Mass.
- J. H. ROGERS, JR., 47 South Third Street, Philadelphia, Penn.
- L. L. BILLINGSLEA, 47 South Third Street, Philadelphia, Penn.
- GEO. D. TELLER, 44 Exchange Street, Buffalo, N. Y.
- D. W. JANOWITZ, Room 1, Jackson Place, Indianapolis, Ind.
- A. A. JACK, 161 Jefferson Avenue, Detroit, Mich.
- T. L. SHORTELL, 104 North Fourth Street, St. Louis, Mo.
- S. H. MILLS, 132 Vine Street, Cincinnati, Ohio.
- T. S. PATTY, 24 West Ninth Street, Chattanooga, Tenn.
- JOHN N. ROBINSON, 392 Broadway, Milwaukee, Wis.
- OSCAR VANDERBILT, 402 Court Avenue, Des Moines, Iowa.
- W. F. SHERWIN, Elmira, N. Y.
- THOS. HENRY, 154 St. James Street, Montreal, Canada.
- THOS. RIDGEDALE, 64 Bay Street, Toronto, Ont.
- T. D. CAMPBELL, 144 Superior Street, Cleveland, Ohio.
- C. G. LEMMON, Friedrich's Hotel, Peoria, Ill.
- FRANK O'NEILL, 121 First Street, Portland, Ore.
- W. N. MEARS, 621 Pacific Avenue, Tacoma, Wash.
- T. K. STATELER, 618 Market Street, San Francisco, Cal.
- W. H. WHITAKER, St. Paul, Minn.

J. M. HANNAFORD,
Traffic Manager.

ST. PAUL, MINN.

CHAS. S. FEE,
General Passenger and Ticket Agent.

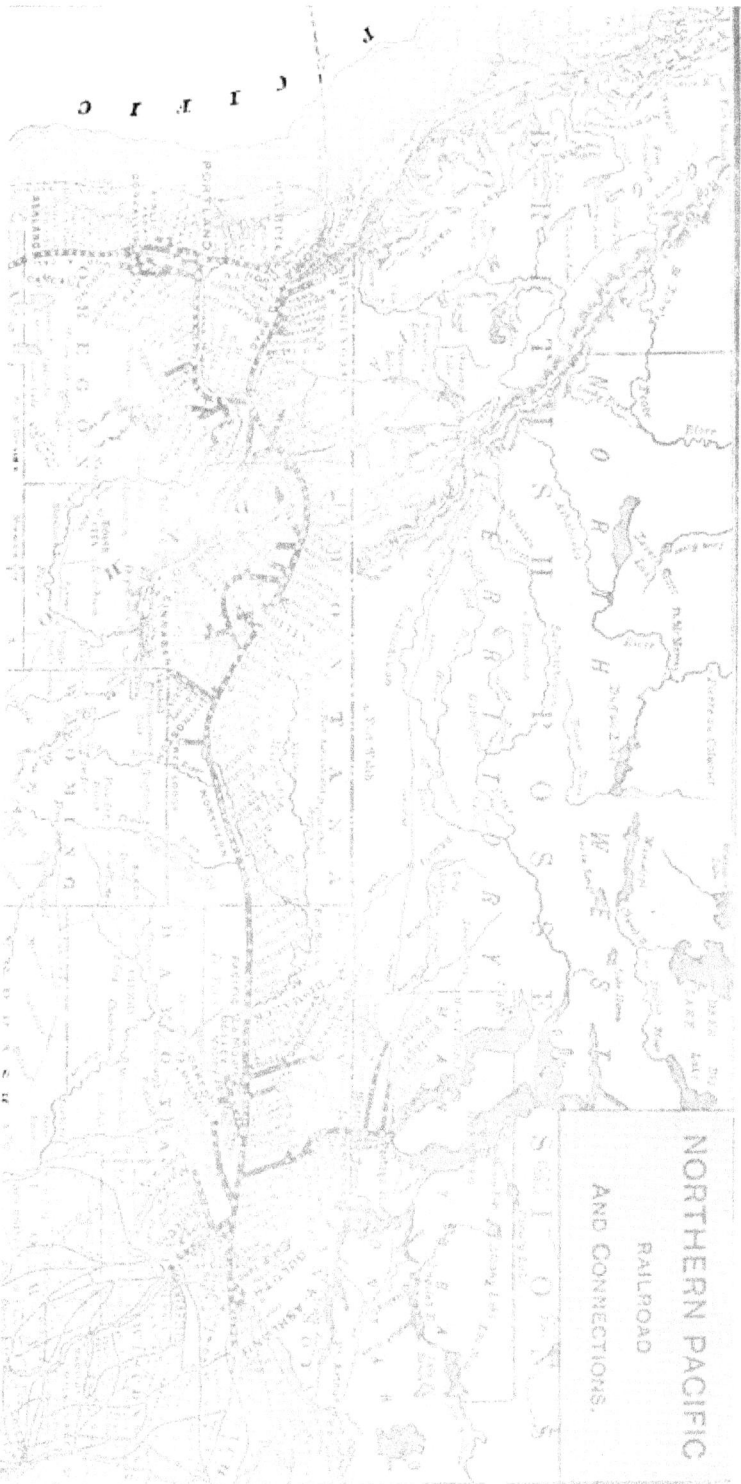
NORTHERN PACIFIC RAILROAD AND CONNECTIONS.

www.ingramcontent.com/pod-product-compliance
Lightning Source LLC
Chambersburg PA
CBHW021408090426
42742CB00009B/1057